Malte Philipp Armbruster

Towards a Reference-Model for Interaction Oriented Systems

Malte Philipp Armbruster

Towards a Reference-Model for Interaction Oriented Systems

Following a perspective based approach to holistic system-modeling in the domain of interaction oriented systems

Südwestdeutscher Verlag für Hochschulschriften

Impressum/Imprint (nur für Deutschland/only for Germany)
Bibliografische Information der Deutschen Nationalbibliothek: Die Deutsche Nationalbibliothek verzeichnet diese Publikation in der Deutschen Nationalbibliografie; detaillierte bibliografische Daten sind im Internet über http://dnb.d-nb.de abrufbar.
Alle in diesem Buch genannten Marken und Produktnamen unterliegen warenzeichen-, marken- oder patentrechtlichem Schutz bzw. sind Warenzeichen oder eingetragene Warenzeichen der jeweiligen Inhaber. Die Wiedergabe von Marken, Produktnamen, Gebrauchsnamen, Handelsnamen, Warenbezeichnungen u.s.w. in diesem Werk berechtigt auch ohne besondere Kennzeichnung nicht zu der Annahme, dass solche Namen im Sinne der Warenzeichen- und Markenschutzgesetzgebung als frei zu betrachten wären und daher von jedermann benutzt werden dürften.

Coverbild: www.ingimage.com

Verlag: Südwestdeutscher Verlag für Hochschulschriften GmbH & Co. KG
Dudweiler Landstr. 99, 66123 Saarbrücken, Deutschland
Telefon +49 681 37 20 271-1, Telefax +49 681 37 20 271-0
Email: info@svh-verlag.de

Approved by: Berlin, TU, Diss., 2011

Herstellung in Deutschland:
Schaltungsdienst Lange o.H.G., Berlin
Books on Demand GmbH, Norderstedt
Reha GmbH, Saarbrücken
Amazon Distribution GmbH, Leipzig
ISBN: 978-3-8381-2773-6

Imprint (only for USA, GB)
Bibliographic information published by the Deutsche Nationalbibliothek: The Deutsche Nationalbibliothek lists this publication in the Deutsche Nationalbibliografie; detailed bibliographic data are available in the Internet at http://dnb.d-nb.de.
Any brand names and product names mentioned in this book are subject to trademark, brand or patent protection and are trademarks or registered trademarks of their respective holders. The use of brand names, product names, common names, trade names, product descriptions etc. even without a particular marking in this works is in no way to be construed to mean that such names may be regarded as unrestricted in respect of trademark and brand protection legislation and could thus be used by anyone.

Cover image: www.ingimage.com

Publisher: Südwestdeutscher Verlag für Hochschulschriften GmbH & Co. KG
Dudweiler Landstr. 99, 66123 Saarbrücken, Germany
Phone +49 681 37 20 271-1, Fax +49 681 37 20 271-0
Email: info@svh-verlag.de

Printed in the U.S.A.
Printed in the U.K. by (see last page)
ISBN: 978-3-8381-2773-6

Copyright © 2011 by the author and Südwestdeutscher Verlag für Hochschulschriften GmbH & Co. KG and licensors
All rights reserved. Saarbrücken 2011

ABSTRACT

One of the latest and most significant challenges in the domain of software development is the successful realization of good usability of the systems generated by this domain. Given the results of conducted surveys regarding the economical costs caused by a lack of software system's user friendliness this trend is easily comprehensible and the inevitable consequence. However, the prevalent models in the domain of software engineering do not sufficiently reflect the aspects of good usability. Thus it is often not possible to include the knowledge and expertise offered by usability experts and designers into the development process of software systems.

To rise to that challenge this work proposes the structure and essential content for a reference model for interaction oriented systems, in an attempt to offer a fundamental, conceptual basis for an encompassing, interdisciplinary model in the domain of software development for human-computer-interaction.

One of the main challenges regarding the construction of that model is being posed by the systemic character of good usability, which is prohibitive of a purely reductionist approach. Rather, during the conceptual work of the construction of the model concepts must be accessed which have proven to be capable tools in the context of systemic modeling. One of these is the concept of a multiple perspective based inspection of a system, which is being reflected in the structure of the model brought forward in this work.

The development process of this model follows a rational and analytical approach and is being anchored in the guidelines, experiences, and suggestions of acknowledged experts in the field of usability, to finally construct a model structure based on three perspectives. This then enables the independent description of a system from the functionality, interaction, and design perspective, thus preparing the ground for the necessary, interdisciplinary dialog. To secure a solid foundation for the model introduced in this work, the Reference Model of Open Distributed Processing (RM-ODP) is being drawn upon.

The practical relevance of the *Reference Model for Interaction Oriented Systems* (RM-IOS) is then being verified during the conduction of a case study which serves as a proof of concept of the goals formulated in the hypothesis.

Contents

List of Figures	X
List of Tables	XII
List of Abbreviations	XIV
1 Introduction	**1**
1.1 Problem statement	2
1.2 Hypothesis	3
1.3 Approach	4
1.4 Structure of this Book	5
2 Preparing Thoughts	**7**
2.1 Model	7
2.1.1 The "Model" term	7
2.2 System	10
2.2.1 Software Systems	13
2.3 Separation of Concern	15
2.3.1 Division of Responsibility and Division of Labor	16
2.3.2 Separation of Concern in Software Systems	18
3 State of the Art	**24**
3.1 Reference Models in UI Development	25

3.2	Models in the Domain of Software Engineering for the User Interface Development		26
3.3	Models and Methodologies for the MDD Approach in UI Development		28
	3.3.1	Model View Controller	29
	3.3.2	Unified Modeling Language	31
	3.3.3	RM-ODP	35
	3.3.4	UsiXML	36
	3.3.5	UMLi	37
	3.3.6	GOMS	38
3.4	Dialog Models		38
	3.4.1	Backus-Naur Form (BNF) grammars	38
	3.4.2	State Transition Diagrams	39
	3.4.3	Statecharts	39
	3.4.4	Petri Nets	40
3.5	ISO Standards Relevant to UI Development		40
	3.5.1	ISO 13407	40
	3.5.2	ISO 9241	41
	3.5.3	ISO 9126	41
	3.5.4	ISO 25000	42
3.6	Conclusion		43

4 Development and Overview of the RM-IOS   **44**

4.1	Motivation		45
4.2	Development of the Model		46
	4.2.1	Towards a Reference Model for Interaction Oriented Systems	47
		Shneiderman's Eight Golden Rules of Interface Design	47
		Collecting Relevant Aspects	50
		Structuring Relevant Aspects	51
		Grouping Relevant Aspects	54
		Selecting Relevant Aspects	56
4.3	RM-IOS - Description		59

		4.3.1	RM-IOS - Foundation	60
		4.3.2	RM-IOS - Functionality	61
		4.3.3	RM-IOS - Interaction	62
		4.3.4	RM-IOS - Style	63
		4.3.5	Coverage of the RM-IOS	64
	4.4	RM-IOS - Six Questions for a Model		65
		4.4.1	Questions for a model	66
			What is RM-IOS a model of?	67
			What is RM-IOS a model for?	68
			Who is RM-IOS for?	68
			Whom is RM-IOS from?	69
			What is RM-IOS' problem domain?	69
			What is RM-IOS' solution domain?	70

5 Reference Model for Interaction Oriented Systems   71

   5.1 RM-IOS 71

   5.2 Foundation 71

   5.3 Functionality Viewpoint 83

   5.4 Interaction Viewpoint 86

   5.5 Style Viewpoint 95

   5.6 Structural UML Class Diagrams of RM-IOS 107

   5.7 Conclusion 112

6 Case Study   114

	6.1	Case Study		114
	6.2	Case Study - Data Collection		118
		6.2.1	Technical Data	118
		6.2.2	Case Study Method	118
			This Case Study's Approach	119
			RM-IOS Elements Used From Each Perspective	119

		Collection of the Data	121
	6.2.3	Data Types in the Case Study	123
		Trigger	124
		String	124
		Expressive Text	125
		Contact	125
		Date	125
		Graphic	125
		Mark	125
6.3	Pre		127
	6.3.1	Functionality	127
		Input	127
		Output	128
	6.3.2	Interaction	128
		Input	128
		Output	129
	6.3.3	Style	130
		Input	130
		Output	130
6.4	iPhone		133
	6.4.1	Functionality	133
		Input	133
		Output	134
	6.4.2	Interaction	134
		Input	134
		Output	135
	6.4.3	Style	135
		Input	135
		Output	136

6.5	Comparison		136
	6.5.1	Functionality	138
		Input	138
		Output	138
	6.5.2	Interaction	139
		Input	139
		Output	140
	6.5.3	Style	141
	6.5.4	Input	141
		Output	142
6.6	Conclusion		144
	6.6.1	Feedback for the Reference Model for Interaction Oriented Systems	145
		Scene	145
		Mode of Operation and Mode of Presentation	146
		Equilibrioceptic Interaction	146
		Minimum Value and Maximum Value	146
6.7	Evaluation of the Case Study		147
	6.7.1	Evaluation in Regard to the Inspected Scenes	147
		Comparison of the Pre's and iPhone's Scene	147
	6.7.2	Evaluation in Regard to the RM-IOS	150
		Policy of Separation of Concern	150
		Provision of Methodological Ground	151

7 Conclusion 153

7.1	Summary of Contributions		153
	7.1.1	Contributions - From the Analytical Perspective	154
		Description	154
		Comparison	154
		Verification	154
		Evaluation	155

	7.1.2	Contributions - From the Synthetical Perspective 155
		Specification 155
	7.1.3	Modeling 155
	7.1.4	Internal Validation 156
	7.1.5	External Validation 157
7.2	Future Work in Prospect 159	
7.3	Scientific Challenges 160	

Bibliography   **169**

List of Figures

3.1 Model-View-Controller Concept 29
3.2 The fourteen diagram types of UML 2.3 represented by a UML class diagram. . . . 32
3.3 Example of Backus-Naur-Form 39

4.1 Aspects of a contemporary IOS 52
4.2 Aspects of a contemporary IOS and their relations 54
4.3 Aspects of a contemporary IOS grouped by colors - 1 56
4.4 Aspects of a contemporary IOS grouped by colors - 2 57
4.5 RM-IOS Architecture 64

5.1 RM-IOS Foundation - UML Class Diagram 108
5.2 RM-IOS Functionality - UML Class Diagram 109
5.3 RM-IOS Interaction - UML Class Diagram 110
5.4 RM-IOS Style - UML Class Diagram 111

6.1 Screenshots of the Pre and iPhone for the Case Study 120
6.2 Structure of the Data Collected in the Case Study 122

List of Tables

4.1	RM-IOS' Perspectives in Galitz' Approach to UI Development	66
6.1	Case Study - Technical Data	119
6.2	Pre - Data Input and Input Type (Functionality Input)	127
6.3	Pre - Data Output and Output Type (Functionality Output)	128
6.4	Pre - Modality and Mode of Operation (Interaction Input)	129
6.5	Pre - Modality and Mode of Presentation (Interaction Output)	130
6.6	Pre (Style Input)	131
6.7	Pre (Style Output)	132
6.8	iPhone - Data Input and Input Type (Functionality Input)	133
6.9	iPhone - Data Output and Output Type (Functionality Output)	134
6.10	iPhone - Modality and Mode of Operation (Interaction Input)	135
6.11	iPhone - Modality and Mode of Presentation (Interaction Output)	136
6.12	iPhone (Style Input)	137
6.13	iPhone (Style Output)	137
6.14	Pre - iPhone (Functionality Input)	139
6.15	Pre - iPhone (Functionality Output)	140
6.16	Pre - iPhone (Interaction Input)	141
6.17	Pre - iPhone (Interaction Output)	142
6.18	Pre - iPhone (Style Input)	143
6.19	Pre - iPhone (Style Output)	144

"Because every person knows what he likes, every person thinks he is an expert on user interfaces."

Paul Heckel, 1982

Chapter 1

Introduction

In the early days of software, when calculations were done based on algorithms read from punchcards, the biggest concern was the correctness of the software. Scientists firmly rooted in mathematical backgrounds were, both, programmer and user in one person and dove into the pool of new found, immense calculating power provided by the computers. As with all ground breaking technologies, here as well the aspect of "usability" - let alone "intuitiveness" - was of absolutely minimal concern. Again, the main challenge was lying in the software delivering correct results at all. That situation has evolved and changed dramatically, as today the calculating power of modern home-computers often exceed the actual demand of the software running on them and the total user base comprises all age groups, all professions, all educational backgrounds, all aspects from casual entertainment to professional applications, and has penetrated almost all aspects of our daily lives. And no longer is the programmer the only user of its own system, quite the opposite is true: very rarely is the developer also the designated user of the software and hardly any end-user implements their own software.

As a consequence of this situation so radically different from the early days of computing, the aspect of usability has already become one of the main challenges and often finds itself to be the key criterion in modern applications or software controlled devices. The way software is being designed and developed, however, does not sufficiently reflect this new situation, effectively leaving the huge and complex task to deliver correctly working and - so called - intuitively usable software to the "the computer scientist" or "the software engineer" to tackle. But as a task complex enough to spawn new faculties at universities falls on the shoulders of people whose expertise lies in different fields, the result of this situation is often unsatisfying as can be seen from products that fail on the market

Introduction   CHAPTER 1

- recently most often because of usability issues and complaints by the end-user about interactions too cumbersome to learn, too annoying to perform frequently, or too restricting. Looking at some of the most established concepts and paradigms in the software development domain sheds some light on this apparent deficit as they stem from a time where the main challenge and thus the focus was still lying in producing correct and reliable software.

In order to rise to the challenge posed by the "as-is" situation just depicted it seems sensible to approach it from a meta level, scrutinizing software design and development as a holistic process while assuming different positions to better understand the currently present discrepancies in skill and requirement from the people and methodologies involved in the entire process.

1.1 Problem statement

An obviously inherent side-effect of the evolution of technical systems is the increase in complexity of these. Software engineering as a discipline dealing with a special kind of technical system, namely software systems, faces the same challenge of increasing complexity as a result of an increase in functional complexity and expected quality in user interaction. Examples for the latter point are the broadening user base of software applications, the penetration of business processes by software, the daily confrontation with software in common situations. Thus the development of today's modern software systems require well organized developing teams with appropriate and able tools, and efficient methodologies to manage the complexity of software development projects and increase the chance of a successful outcome [AMB+04].

It is, however, a widely acknowledged fact in the software industry that actually only a minority of software projects result in a satisfying product in terms of time taken from conception to the release of the application, staying within the development budget, or meeting the client's expectations in terms of functionality and usability [SP05][Cha09][RG01].

While several aspects are relevant to this problem recently especially the issue of usability and interaction design has received increased attention from, both, the developer and the client side, as some ads and slogans from large manufacturers of heavily software rooted technical devices – for example Philips' "Sense and Simplicity" [Phi09] – also give testament to.

One fundamentally important and enabling technique in the evolution of technology is the development of a well defined policy of "separation of concern", allowing for the increasing mass of knowledge in a discipline to be distributed into distinct sets of chunks defined by describing uniting and distinguishing attributes. This allows for specialization and levels of expertise otherwise not feasible if all comprised in one discipline.

In software, however, a distinct difference to other traditional engineering disciplines is the circumstance that the fundamental building blocks are not tangible materials but source code, thus not offering a natural separation of concern based on subfields specialized in the handling of certain material [RS08]. But several techniques exist where a policy of separation of concern has been introduced into software engineering with great success. Examples are the object-oriented programming (OOP) paradigm in programming and system architecture, the model-view-controller (MVC) pattern in GUI oriented programming, or the extensive reference model for open distributed processing (RM-ODP) in the development of open distributed systems. All these techniques have provided − over the time they have been applied − empirical evidence that they allow for more complex systems to be successfully developed and maintained. Yet, none of the existing patterns regard the increasingly important aspect of usability and interactability with sufficient distinction [CRC07] [SP05] [Ras07]. These three cornerstones of the evolution of software design and development will be discussed in regard to their inclusion of usability aspects - or lack thereof - very briefly in chapter 2 and then more thoroughly in 3.

1.2 Hypothesis

It is possible to develop a perspective based reference-model defining a policy of separation of concern applicable to software design and development in the segment of interaction with the following effects:

- mirroring the separated domains of skill, knowledge, and expertise required to cope with the needs of successful interaction design and implementation

- covering the many aspects to be dealt with in successful interaction design and implementation

- providing methodological ground for analysis and evaluation of existing interaction solutions

- providing the basis for proper organization of development teams for interaction design and implementation

- it can be justified by what is known about successful interaction design and implementation endeavors.

Assumptions

This hypothesis is based on two assumptions. Namely, the first assumption, that it is possible and sensible to separate the domain of software design and development into distinct sub-domains. This assumption is based on observing comparable separations in other domains, such as engineering disciplines and construction workflows where measurable advantages have been reached. Based on the established first assumption the following second assumption then is that a separation of the domain of software design and development into the sub-domains of "functionality", "interaction", and "style" aspects gives reason to believe to be meeting many of the points listed above.

1.3 Approach

In this book the points listed in the hypothesis (1.2) will be answered by constructing a reference-model describing three distinct viewpoints.

Namely the viewpoint containing the concerns of the provided functionality of a software system, the viewpoint containing the interaction and usability concerns of a software system, and the viewpoint containing the concerns relevant to aesthetic design decisions.

The description of these three viewpoints then provide a meta-framework for conceptualizing, inspecting, and analyzing software systems while appreciating the different domains of skill, knowledge, and expertise that each stems from. Furthermore it acknowledges the growing importance of usability and interaction concerns and provides the semantic lens to focus on these challenges in modern software systems.

However, it has to be acknowledged, that it is - per definition - impossible to provide empirical justification for the development of a model as just described during the course of a thesis. To cope with this a rational approach must be followed in assuring that the model fulfills the points established in the hypothesis.

During the course of this thesis it will be attempted to present and justify these two assumptions made in the hypothesis in a comprehensible and traceable manner to then apply the consequences arising from them to the domain of software design and development with the intent to describe a reference model meeting the points listed in the hypothesis (1.2).

1.4 Structure of this Book

Chapter 1 - Introduction

Chapter 1 provides the reader with an introduction into the domain of this work and presents the problem statement, the driving motivation for this work. Followed then by the hypothesis, and a description of the approach that was taken in order to verify the hypothesis.

Chapter 2 - Preparing Thoughts

Chapter 2 introduces the fundamental underlying concepts of this work, namely the concept of a model and the concept of a system in order to prepare some common mental ground on which to build the rest of the work. The approach of this chapter is a top-down approach, i.e. the two concepts are viewed at first from a general perspective and are then refined and specified to the point of view taken by this work. Consequently the following chapters build on top of the terms and concepts identified and defined in this chapter.

Chapter 3 - State of the Art

Chapter 3 presents and discusses the current state of the art in the domain of software design and development in the field of user interface engineering. It is the goal of this chapter to give the reader a sufficient overview of some of the currently applied models and methodologies in respect to the problem statement and hypothesis presented in the introduction (1.1 and 1.2). Together with the problem statement and the hypothesis, the current state of the art provides the third anchorpoint to identify the contribution made by this work.

Chapter 4 - Development and Overview of the RM-IOS

Chapter 4 lays out the analytical development process that preceded and lead to the development of the Reference Model for Interaction Oriented Systems. Part of this chapter are furthermore summarizing descriptions of the model and the answer to six fundamental questions any model can be asked.

Chapter 5 - Reference Model for Interaction Oriented Systems

Chapter 5 then presents the Reference Model for Interaction Oriented Systems that has been designed and constructed in order to answer to the challenges posed by the problem statement and substantiated by the hypothesis. It is the result of following the approach described in chapter 4. The Reference Model for Interaction Oriented Systems describes three point of views, that of the functionality of a software ("*What* can a user do?"), that of the interaction between a software and the user ("*How* does a user access the functionality?"), and that of the style of the possible interaction ("How are the interaction possibilities being presented to the user?").

Chapter 6 - Case Study

Chapter 6 demonstrates a practical application of the Reference Model for Interaction Oriented Systems by analyzing typical activities performed with two different, state of the art smartphones (the Palm Pre and the Apple iPhone). By subjecting the same activity on each different device to the same analysis technique based on the Reference Model for Interaction Oriented Systems a first impression is being offered to the analytical value of the Reference Model for Interaction Oriented Systems.

While it is sensible to assume that the Reference Model for Interaction Oriented Systems could also be of value to the synthesis of software a demonstration of such synthesis will not be part of this work for several reasons, mainly the following two: Firstly, any software synthesis beyond the most trivial level requires significant time and resources and secondly, the synthesis of software, especially the synthesis in accordance with this Reference Model for Interaction Oriented Systems would require expertise in all three areas, i.e. the area of functionality, interaction-design, and style-design. The combination of these two aspects made a case-study focusing on the synthesis value of the Reference Model for Interaction Oriented Systems impossible during the course of the writing of this work.

Chapter 7 - Conclusion

Chapter 6 presents the conclusions of this work and the contributions made. It also discusses the scientific outlook and offers ideas for work that could build on the basis of this work.

Chapter 2

Preparing Thoughts

Before it is possible to think about any kind of separation of an entity, the whole entity must be viewed and inspected with the goal to find out about its nature and characteristic attributes relevant for the kind of intended separation. The intended separation in this thesis will be the establishing of perspectives based on the domains of skill, knowledge, and expertise of the designers and developers involved in the user interface development process. Hence the whole, i.e. the domain of software design and development in user interface development must be viewed and approached thusly, that the just mentioned segments become mentally visible and tangible.

In preparation of this the fundamental terms must be identified and defined as used and to be understood throughout this thesis. This chapter introduces these terms and follows a top-down approach: providing at first a very general view on a term to then narrow down on the term, focusing on the term with the semantic lense of this thesis' domain to finally provide a definitive description, making the term useful to communicate the concepts needed for this thesis.

2.1 Model

2.1.1 The "Model" term

The chapter will begin with a clarification of the "model" term in order to establish a common understanding of the term as it will be used throughout this thesis and this chapter especially. Then the motivation regarding the usefulness or even necessity of models is being presented; first from a more general point of view, then narrowed down to why models are useful and necessary in the context of the particular domain this model is being introduced into, namely the domain of software design and development.

Stachowiak and Mahr

The term "model" is prevalently used and heavily overloaded as discussed in great detail by Mahr in [Mah03]. In this article Mahr first illuminates the complex etymological history of the term "model" and soon concludes, that the "modelness" of a model is not something that can be found in any of the model's attributes, but rather must be identified in the pragmatic context, in which the decision is being made to perceive something *as* a model. This is a stark distinction from the usually accepted definition of a model in technical domains which is based on Stachowiak's definition who stipulates three attributes *a model must possess* [Sta73]. A good translation and further inspection of this definition of a model and its role in the model driven development can be found in Kühne's article "What is a Model?" [Küh05]:

1. mapping feature - a model is based on an original
2. reduction feature - a model only reflects a (relevant) selection of the original's properties
3. pragmatic feature - a model needs to [be] usable in place of the original with respect to some purpose

To locate the "modelness" of a model in either in some attributes of the model itself or in the context of perception of whomever perceives a model as a model is the most fundamental difference between Stachowiak's and Mahr's definition of a model. Following Mahr's argumentation in [Mah03] the following thoughts can be extracted:

Vitruv and the Proportions

In the historic context of the model where Vitruv uses the model as a tool to express what he must obviously perceive as the essence of architecture, namely the proportions and symmetry of a structure, a striking similarity can be identified in the use of models in today's information technology where models are used to express the essence of software systems; often from several different perspectives as the complexity of contemporary software systems demands.

In his contemplations of the model, Mahr also raises the question exactly how useful a model (in the Vitruvian context of architecture) can be to produce beauty and lead to the realization of aesthetic ideals, when it merely contains numbers regarding the proportions of the architecture. It must then be deduced that in regard to the perceived beauty of the building the, say, color of the building was not nearly as important as the proportion of its elements. The details worked into the facade of the building possibly only artistic expressions of the builder not fundamental aspects of the structure's beauty. The essence of the ideal of beauty and aesthetic was identified in the proportions of the building and thus this is the aspect captured and transmitted in the Vitruvian concept of the model. And here the similarity to the nature of models and their conception and use in the context of contemporary software development can be extended even further, as a model of a software system never contains an explicit description of, say, the actual source code to be implemented. It contains merely those aspects perceived as being of fundamental importance to the defining characteristics of that particular software and its architecture. The actual source code, the way a developer comments the code, even the details of the algorithms implemented to realize the functionality required from the system, and aesthetic aspects whether the curly braces of function calls are placed on the same line of the function's name or on the next are simply relinquished to the personal preference of the developer[1]; much as the aspects of a building not captured in the Vitruvian model are relinquished to the builder's personal preference.

It can be concluded, then, that in the models provided for and by a discipline, and used by a discipline an unambiguous inference can be drawn about what is being perceived as essential aspects to that discipline, i.e. aspects perceived as fundamentally crucial; important enough to be included in the models of its artifacts. Thus, inspecting the models currently prevalent in the domain of software development some insight should be gained about where the priorities of that discipline lie. This inspection will be done in chapter 3.

Models as a Lense of a Discipline's Focus

Mahr continues and mentions Dürer, who failed in his attempt of capturing the beauty of the human body by merely referring to the proportions of it and subsequently expressed this apparently disappointing realization with the words "Waß aber dy schonheit sey, daz weis jch nit." [Win71, p. 61], which translates into: "but what beauty is, that I do not know". Mahr then draws the acute conclusion that the models used by a discipline can be a limiting factor on the perception of the discipline regarding the entities it is occupied with. Another parallel can be drawn to the lack of

---

[1] This may not always be the case when large groups of developers work on the same code and maximum legibility must be obtained. But this leads into another direction entirely.

usability related aspects in the prevalent models used in the domain of software engineering and the lack of good usability in contemporary software systems; more on that, also, in chapter 3.

Summarizing Thoughts on the Model

In this article Mahr formulates the concept of a model always being a *model of* something and a *model for* something (a thought which Mahr then extends to the concept of the "cargo of a model" in [Mah09], however, this continuative concept is not necessary for this thesis).

It can be said, that models in general are a fundamental component to a discipline and the nature of models determines and are a mirror of the nature of thoughts a discipline preoccupies itself with. And the discipline of information science relies particularly strongly on models and their expressive power (for an in-depth discussion of this thought refer to Mahr's article "Information science and the logic of models" [Mah09]).

In accordance with Mahr's conceptual nature of a model, the model introduced in this thesis is being defined by answering to the questions "what is this model a model of" and "what is this model a model for". The answers to these two questions, along with answers to other questions that are also relevant to this model, will be given in section 4.4.

2.2 System

The etymological root of the word "system" is the greek word *"systema"* which in turn comprises the two greek words "syn" (together) and "histemi" (put) and thus describes a whole which consists of parts. Due to this high-level and extremely generic meaning of the word, it can be found used in almost any context, i.e. the "nervous system" in the medical context, the "financial system" in an economic context, the "health-care system" in the public health context, the "system of intervals" in the music-theory context, or the "computer system" in the technological context, to name just a few.

Aristotle and Metaphysics

The first recorded philosophic usage of the word can be found in Plato's dialog "Philebus" from 360 B.C. [PlaBC] where he applies the term "system" to describe (musical) intervals and their relation to one another.

> But when you have learned what sounds are high and what low, and the number and nature of the intervals and their limits or proportions, and the *systems* compounded out of them, which our fathers discovered, and have handed down to us who are their descendants under the name of harmonies [...]

But Plato and Aristotle also apply the term "system" to describe a federation of states and within the hellenistic school of thought the Stoics make use of the term to describe the cosmos as a physical *system* of the heavens and the earth and the creatures in between [Mar98]. Possibly the most well known quote about systems and their special nature comes from Aristotle in his work Metaphysics where he states "the whole is more than the sum of its parts [Ari91]" giving word to the concept of a system's "emerging properties". Then throughout history the term system is being used ubiquitously in any context.

Descartes and Reductionism

A turning point in the thinking of and about systems was the reductionist school of thought, with Rene Descartes being one of its most prominent thinkers. Descartes held the belief, that a system and its properties is no more than the sum of the properties of its parts [Des37]. This was a stark contrast to the aristotelean view of a system being *more* than the sum of its parts.

von Bertalanffy and General Systems Theory

Returning to the aristotelean view on systems (regarding the interdependent complexity of its parts) it was the biologist Ludwig von Bertalanffy who laid the foundation for the establishing of "systems theory" as a scientific discipline with his influential book on the thinking of and about systems, which was published in the year 1976. The book is titled "General Systems Theory" [vB76] and in it von Bertalanffy strives to establish a theory for thinking about and working with systems in an abstract and general way and returns to the principle of "emerging properties", i.e. properties of a system that are not present in any of its parts individually but only *come to be* in their systemic liaison[2].

---

[2]It is interesting that the concept of an emerging property can be described particularly well with musical intervals, which is the context from which Plato's and Aristotle's use of the term "system" stems. When such an interval of two tones sounds, it is extremely difficult for the untrained ear to identify the two sounds that produce the sound of the interval. The individual tones merge together to form the characteristic sound of that interval,

Preparing Thoughts CHAPTER 2

Perspectives on a System

This line of thought can be extended to the possibility of inspecting a system in different ways in such a manner, that certain aspects of the system come to the fore, whereas other aspects of the system fade out into the background. These aspects can then be grouped by associating characteristics and such a group of aspects and their defining, associating characteristic can then be considered a *perspective on the system*. For example, it is possible to inspect the physical composition of a device, where the materials used, their color, shape, and texture would be the focus of interest. Or the same device could be inspected from a historic perspective, where the era of time the device was being used is of interest. Note, that in this case the inspected aspect can not be found *in* or *on* the device itself, but rather in the context of the device. To conclude this example, the same device could be inspected from a perspective of its functionality, where the chief interest would be the answering of the question "what is this device for?".

This concept of a perspective based inspection of a system is a powerful tool in the analysis and description of systems as it does not disrupt the holistic nature of a system and recognizes the nature of emerging properties of a system while at the same time allowing for a reduction in perceived complexity of the system.

The concept of a perspective based inspection of a system is a core concept of the model introduced in this thesis and will thus resurface again.

Description of a System

At the same time it is clear that a system can only be described by the use of a model [Mah09]. Whether that model is a prosaic description of the system, a graphical representation of the system, or even a physical representation of the system; all those are models of the system to be described.

---

where the individual tones themselves become less present to the listener and the characteristic sound of the interval emerges. The characteristic sound of the interval here is an *emerging property* of the two sounds in the interval as that characteristic sound of the interval is not present in either of the two tones by themselves but only in their combination it becomes audible. Continuing this line of thought a melody also is an *emerging property* of the underlying tones. Even more complex, then, the symphony as a grand example of an emerging property, where individual sounds, even individual instruments become secondary to the sound of the melody and harmonic structure *emerging* from their combination as its *emerging property*.

It appears almost paradoxical that even the duplication of a system for the sake of describing the system can only be considered a 1:1 *model of the described system* as the identity of the two systems is obviously not the same[3].

"General Systems Theory" Pervasion

The principle of "systemic thinking" then pervaded a plethora of disciplines, among others for example the living systems theory (for example see [MM92]), sociology and sociocybernetics (for example see [Buc68]), organizational theory (for examples see [Sen94] and [Che99]), and also the domain of software and computing where Vaughn Frick and Albert F. Case, Jr. brought forward the transformation from "system analysis" to "system design" [Jr.85].

Summarizing Thoughts on Systems

Summarizing this brief overview the following points can be retained.

1. The system term is being used ubiquitously.
2. A system is a composed whole, consisting of components, which in turn can be systems themselves.
3. Systems theory has pervaded and influenced a plethora of disciplines.
4. A system can be viewed from different viewpoints.
5. A system can only be described by the use of (a) model(s).

The following section then takes a closer look at the "system" term in the domain of software systems.

2.2.1 Software Systems

A software system is a system based on software.

---

[3]This point re-illustrates the argument of Mahr [Mah08] that it is the *intention* by someone to perceive something as a model that makes a model a model and nothing in the actual attributes of the model itself that could make it a model.

This definition seems so trivial that it appears self-evident and quite useless. However, after careful consideration of the term "software system" several aspects become apparent which make the definition of software systems anything but trivial.

The first aspect would regard the inherently necessary relationship of software to some hardware, as software can not run (exist?) without hardware. While the algorithm of some software can of course be written down on a piece of paper, essentially representing the functional essence of the software, nobody would actually call those scribblings a software system. Also the text files containing the source code in whichever programming language are not a software system. Then the source code is being compiled into a machine processable form. At this point now there are a number of files stored, for example, on the hard-drive of a computer containing machine processible instructions. But still this collection of files is not going to be considered a software system.

Upon loading of the executable file on the hard-drive the instructions contained within these files are being executed by the processor, and the relevant parts of the machine processible code is being loaded into the registers of the CPU, the cache-memory of the CPU, and the random-access-memory (RAM) of the computer.

The difference in voltage on the circuit board of the computer caused by the executed instructions of the program files is the physical presence of the program being currently run, however, that physical presence would not be considered a software system at all, but instead, the perceivable effect of that physical presence, namely, the output the system generates and provides to the user – usually based on whichever input the user has provided the system with – would commonly be regarded as a software system.

Albeit, the average end-user of a software-system typically has a completely different conception of a software-system than the developer who wrote the source code, or the software engineer who designed its architecture. The end-user typically perceives the entire system she interacts with as a "software-system", making no distinction between the hardware-system she interacts with (in order to receive output from the software-system and provide input to the software-system) and the actual software-system that is being run by the hardware-system. If a smartphone's microphone is dysfunctional *"the phone is broken"*, and if a smartphone's operating system does not boot anymore due to some error in the code *"the phone is broken"*.

This somewhat naïve view on a (software-)system is actually of fundamental importance when considering the aspect of usability, as it demonstrates quite perfectly that the usability and user-friendliness of a (software-)system does not only depend on the software itself, but the control elements of the (hardware-) system just as much.

Emerging Usability

Additionally the "usability" or "user-friendliness" of a system must be identified as an emerging property of the system, as if it was not, then it would have to be an attribute that can be found in one of the components of the system. But the fact of the matter is, that this is precisely not the case. If good usability could be recognized from a component of the system, then achieving good usability would be easy as one would simply have to imbue the elements of a system with good usabilty and this attribute would then propagate through the system. This is obviously not the case, but instead good usability and user-friendliness is a systemic aspect of the sytem and thus extremely difficult to isolate.

To account for the just presented line of thought, in this thesis the term "software system" is being used to refer to a software application geared towards interaction with a user and also the peripheral hardware elements that provide the means of interacting with the application, i.e. receiving input from the user and presenting output to the user.

Finally, the classification of good usability as an emerging property of a system will be an important aspect in the development process of the Reference Model for Interaction Oriented Systems introduced later on.

2.3 Separation of Concern

Shneiderman states that a software-system, being a complex system, must be viewed as a whole [SP05]. While there is great merit to this holistic approach in terms of the overall design of the application as it acknowledges the nature of good usability as a rather elusive aspect of the system, the examination of a sufficiently complex system by its individual parts and their working can not be avoided when trying to design and build it. Furthermore there is historic evidence, that a well realized policy of separation of concern is the key to progress and increase in quality. In order to inspect software systems in regard to the creation of a reference model for interaction oriented system that implements a successful policy of separation of concern based on the different skill sets

Preparing Thoughts CHAPTER 2

required in the domain of user interface development for software systems, the concept of separation of concern will be inspected now.

Separation of concern is a concept that can be applied as a technique or observed as a state. The concept of separation of concern is based on the idea of dividing a whole into at least two or more separately functioning entities with the separation being defined by clearly distinguishing between each entity's responsibility regarding the purpose of the whole. As such it is often found to be a fundamental core concept of the system - the "integrated whole" - principle.

This is obviously not a concept that is exclusive to the technical world of which computer science, software design, development, and programming is a part of but instead can be found ubiquitously in all kinds of systems. For the purpose of this work, however, the focus lies in the meaning of separation of concern in the context of software systems and division of responsibility. In order to illustrate the ideas inherent in the concept of separation of concern first a general and abstract look at separation of concern and its historic context is given.

2.3.1 Division of Responsibility and Division of Labor

When a single task becomes so demanding, either by the complexity of its whole or in knowledge it requires, a concept that has successfully been applied throughout history has been the division of labor and thus enabled concept of specialization. The idea, in short, is that many specialists, with in-depth knowledge of a certain aspect of the whole, working on one solution will be able to produce a superior product over many non-specialists, with general and broad knowledge of all aspects, working on one solution; superior in terms of time needed until completion, degree of sophistication, suitability for its intended purpose, quality of its manufacturing, and so forth. This concept is known as division of responsibility or division of labor. The following sections present a brief historic retrospection on this concept.

Plato and the Republic

The concept of division of responsibility can be traced back to Plato who discusses these thoughts circa 380 B.C. in his socratic dialog "The Republic" where he describes how his idea of a republic will fulfill the needs of its subjects thusly: "Well then, how will our state supply these needs? It will need a farmer, a builder, and a weaver, and also, I think, a shoemaker and one or two others to provide for our bodily needs. So that the minimum state would consist of four or five men...." [4] [Pla07].

Mandeville and the Bee Hive

And even though Mandeville's poem "The Grumbling Hive" in his book "Fable of the Bees" [Man05] is in its essence a social critique, the prosaic discussion he includes contains thoughts on division of responsibility and labor in order to improve the final result: "But if one will wholly apply himself to the making of Bows and Arrows, whilst another provides Food, a third builds Huts, a fourth makes Garments, and a fifth Utensils, they not only become useful to one another, but the Callings and Employments themselves will in the same Number of Years receive much greater Improvements, than if all had been promiscuously followed by every one of the Five." [Man05].

Adam Smith and the Economic Revolution

Adam Smith then places the principle of division of responsibility and labor in the context of the economic revolution of the 18th century with his epic and influential work "An Inquiry into the Nature and Causes of the Wealth of Nations" [Smi76] in which he articulates two fundamental aspects - among others - inherently present in the division of responsibility and labor:

1. The division of responsibility and labor as the fundamental enabling principle to industrial growth, progress, and wealth.
2. The division of responsibility and labor as a "mental mutilation" of the workers due to monotonous, repetitive work which disconnects the worker from the product.

Regarding the second aspect it must be kept in mind, that Smith discusses the principle of division of responsibility and labor in the context of a pin manufacture; not in the context of the mentally highly demanding work of software development. However, this is still an interesting point to be raised when thinking about establishing a policy of separation of concern in the domain of software development. However, it is a matter that must be inspected in the field of psychology rather than during the process of engineering a model.

---

[4]It is interesting to note, that the actual division of labor does not seem to be that particularly striking of a revelation to Plato. Rather, the fact that the combined effort of these individual specialists would be able to supply the needs of the state seems to be the conceptual revelation here.

Preparing Thoughts   CHAPTER 2

Karl Marx and the Enslavement to Work

The drawback of workers losing motivation due to the boring and unfulfilling nature of their completely monotonous (or: extremely specialized) work was then further discussed by Karl Marx. Marx also identifies an element of social hierarchy in the division of labor and warns of a division of responsibility and labor caused by social status rather than technical necessity in his work "Teilung der Arbeit und Manufaktur" ("Division of Labor and Manufacture") [ME68]. This line of thought then lead to the idea of an ideal communist society in which people find fulfillment in the work they do – however, this leads to another topic entirely.

But this brief retrospection shows that the concept of a policy of separation of concern is one that has accompanied any technical progress from the earliest days and - besides the potential drawbacks afore mentioned - lead to improvements in productivity, overall quality of the end-product, and an increase in knowledge gained in the subfields.

At this point now the concept of division of responsibility will be viewed in the context of software systems.

2.3.2 Separation of Concern in Software Systems

The term separation of concern itself was introduced to the realm of software by Edsger W. Dijkstra in his paper "On the role of scientific thought" written in 1974, published in 1982 in his "Selected Writings on Computing: A Personal Perspective"[Dij82] where he writes:

> Let me try to explain to you, what to my taste is characteristic for all intelligent thinking. It is, that one is willing to study in depth an aspect of one's subject matter in isolation for the sake of its own consistency, all the time knowing that one is occupying oneself only with one of the aspects. We know that a program must be correct and we can study it from that viewpoint only; we also know that it should be efficient and we can study its efficiency on another day, so to speak. In another mood we may ask ourselves whether, and if so: why, the program is desirable. But nothing is gained –on the contrary!– by tackling these various aspects simultaneously. It is what I sometimes have called *"the separation of concerns"* which, even if not perfectly possible, is yet the only available technique for effective ordering of one's thoughts, that I know of. This is what I mean by "focusing one's attention upon some aspect": it does not mean ignoring

the other aspects, it is just doing justice to the fact that from this aspect's point of view, the other is irrelevant. It is being one- and multiple-track minded simultaneously.

In the domain of software development then the concept of separation of concern can be observed in two different ways. On the one hand it is a technique that is being applied to the structuring and organization of the elements of a software system in order to achieve modularity, the fundamental essence of modern software development techniques such as the object oriented programming (OOP) paradigm; this will be referred to as the technical level of a software system. On the other hand it is being realized as a concept in the modeling of software projects by having different tools available for modeling a system from different perspectives; this will be referred to as the conceptual level of a software system.

The following part inspects the concept of separation of concern in the domain of software development on the technical level. After that the concept of separation of concern in the domain of software development on the conceptual level will be inspected.

Technical Separation of Concern

The concept of separation of concern has been successfully realized on the technical level of software development. Evidence of this can be found in, for example, the evolution of programming from monolithic code to modular code, then evolving to the object oriented paradigm, which partitions the code architecture of a software system into separate classes which generate objects according to a prescribed specification which in turn encapsulate their attributes and offer their services via public functions. Another example on a more abstract level then is the "Model View Controller" paradigm which takes the concepts of separation of concern even further by defining the arrangement of the classes according to well defined responsibilities, namely the responsibility of data handling (model classes), representation of the data (view classes), and the business logic working on the data (controller classes) (see section 3.3.1 for a more detailed inspection).

The underlying motivation to all these evolvements was the concept of a beneficial realization of a policy of separation of concern. As obviously the question "what is a sensible approach to efficiently partitioning a system in order to reduce the perceived complexity when inspecting it".

An overly simplistic approach could have been to simply segment the entire source code by number of lines of code, i.e. create packages of code, each containing one hundred lines of code. But clearly such an obviously useless approach would cause more confusion and increase the overall complexity and not be helpful at all in reducing it and making it more manageable.

The concept of partitioning a system into parts governed by some underlying principle of commonality of its elements apparently fits with the way the human mind perceives and orders things. It then follows that the concept of separation of concern is an inherent and inseparable part on the technical level of contemporary software development as it provides a powerful concept for reducing the perceived complexity of a system at any given moment by fading some aspects out and bringing other aspects to the front of the attention.

This is only to realize that the concept of separation of concern is very much a part of the technical evolution of the domain of software development in general. The other aspect is the realization of the concept of separation of concern on the conceptual level of the domain of software development. This will now be briefly inspected.

Conceptual Separation of Concern

The term "conceptual separation of concern" is here being used to refer to the aspect in the domain of software development where different areas of knowledge and conceptual segmentation of a software-system is being applied.

One practical example for this is the Unified Modeling Language (UML) which offers several different types of diagrams to describe a system from several different perspectives (see section 3.3.2 for a more detailed inspection). The need for such a modeling language with its flexible descriptive abilities and the undeniable success of UML as the de facto industry standard graphical modeling language for software systems is a clear indicator for the complexity of software-systems and the domain of software development as a discipline.

Another good example for the need of a successfully realized policy of separation of concern on the conceptual level of software development is the Reference Model of Open Distributed Processing (RM-ODP) which in its core offers a vocabulary for the description of open distributed systems from five different perspectives, called viewpoints (see section 3.3.3 for a more detailed inspection). In the RM-ODP foundation the viewpoint is being defined as: "viewpoint (on a system): A form of abstraction achieved using a selected set of architectural concepts and structuring rules, in order to focus on particular concerns within a system." [RO97, Definition 3.2.7]. This is precisely what

Dijkstra described above regarding the fading in and out of relevant and currently irrelevant aspects of a system, only here on a greater scale.

Both, the UML and the RM-ODP, however, were developed to answer to the increasing complexity in contemporary software systems and the challenges thereby posed for the development process. However, the aspect of a software system's usability has so far not been part of a successfully realized policy of separation of concern.

The just briefly expressed thought here serves only the purpose to initially raise the concept of separation of concern in the conceptual level of the domain of software development into the awareness of the reader. A thorough discussion of these concepts and their relevance to this thesis and the herein introduced model follow in chapter 3.

Concluding Thoughts on Division of Responsibility

The domain of user interface development is a vast field comprising several disciplines. Traditionally the discipline of user interface development has been part of the domain of software engineering as the realization of anything "software" fell into the area of responsibility of programmers and software developers.

In the domain of software development the concept of division of responsibility has been introduced successfully on, both, the technical level and the conceptual level. However, the aspect of usability has not been the focus of attention up until very recently.

Also, an interesting peculiarity in the domain of software development in regard to division of responsibility is the fact, that contrary to the manufacture of tangible objects - for example a car - everything implemented in software is virtual and per se does not possess any attributes or behavioral pattern in and by itself. That is to say, that the domain of software development does not lend itself easily to a naturally evident division of responsibility based on expertise in the handling of certain materials as does the domain of tangible product manufacturing. Instead, the division of responsibility in the domain of software is being determined by conceptual differences in the nature of software. For example, there are security specialists, database specialists, specialists for the optimization of code in terms of its speed and memory footprint, and so forth.

Considering then Dijkstra's thoughts on the separation of concern (see 2.3.2) it becomes immediately apparent, that he is describing the very core concept of division of responsibility that allows for the evolution of systems, from simple, often "one-man-built"-systems into grand, complex systems when he says:

> [...]This is what I mean by "focusing one's attention upon some aspect": it does not mean ignoring the other aspects, it is just doing justice to the fact that from this aspect's point of view, the other is irrelevant.[...]

But while Dijkstra describes a single person thinking on different aspects of a system by blending the irrelevant aspects in and out, in modern workflows and workgroups different people are exclusively preoccupied with different aspects of the system.

Since effectual evidence can be found that this process of specialization and division of labor has been successfully applied in other engineering disciplines and also in the discipline of software development itself it is sensible to accept that the process of user interface design and development in the domain of software development would also benefit from such specialization, and division of responsibility and labor, realized by a well defined policy of separation of concern.

Chapter 3

State of the Art

This chapter aims to provide an overview of the current state of the art in user interface development with regard to the relevance of a reference model as introduced in this thesis. In particular, this chapter will demonstrate that in the current landscape of models available to the domain of software development in user interface development there is no reference model as the one introduced in this thesis. Furthermore, this chapter strives to identify the historically[1] founded reasons for the lack of proper support for user interface development in the current array of tools available to the domain of software development.

Reviewing the historic development of the software user interface development domain will help to identify some of the reasons why the aspect of usability is such a problematic and challenging one. To understand the underlying cause for this, the predominant mental tools available to the domain of software engineering must be examined as the tools of a discipline always reveal the nature of and the mental models present in the discipline itself.

This chapter will only briefly cover the different methodological approaches in contemporary user interface design, as for this thesis the methodological approaches are not of central interest. The focus must - and will - instead be on the available and predominant underlying models of the methodologies in the domain of user interface development.

During the course of this chapter it will become apparent, that the focus of attention in the domain of user interface development has been one aligned on the technical aspects and realization, i.e. implementation of a user interface. The other discipline of fundamental importance in the domain

---

[1]The term "historic" here is to be understood in the timeframe of the software development history, which obviously is a very short but furious one.

of user interface development has been the area of cognitive psychology, which when relevant to the domain of human computer interaction is being covered by Shneiderman in his extensive, influential, and constantly updated book "Designing the User Interface" [SP05].

Thus, this chapter will now begin with a brief retrospection on the history of the idea of a reference model for the domain of user interface development.

3.1 Reference Models in UI Development

In order to appreciate the current situation in user interface development of those aspects relevant to the domain of a reference model as introduced in this thesis, it seems prudent to take a look at the historical developments in that field.

The idea of a reference model for the domain of user interface development is not a new one, as exactly this concept has been brought to the attention of the SIGCHI workshop of 1986. In the bulletin of that workshop the lead-article by Lynch and Meads can be found [LM86], in which the need for a common vocabulary to communicate unambiguously across several different disciplines had already been recognized. Unfortunately this thought was quickly being dismissed again:

> We flirted with the idea that our biggest contribution to the whole might be in compiling a common vocabulary or maybe even just learning to talk to each other in some common language. We still feel that this is a valuable task, but for some other group. [LM86]

The article then describes the discussion that took place among the participants of that workshop regarding the question of exactly what a reference model for user interfaces should be which eventually lead to a list of factors regarding the user's interaction with the system that should be supported by a reference model, some of which are rather technical, such as "undo" and "redo", whereas others are rather esoteric, such as "yin/yang" and "warm fuzzies" demonstrating the generally penumbral view on the whole matter.

Another article by Lantz [Lan86] then from the same workshop already is much more concise in its proposition of a possible reference model for user interfaces, but its approach represents a very broad field of aspects. It provides suggestions of factors a "good interface" should include, attempting to express the user's interaction with the system in linguistic terms such as lexical, syntactical, and semantical level[2], and inspecting the role of the dialogue manager in order to deal with multiple workstation agents. The conference concludes without any concrete proposition of a reference model for user interfaces but invites contributions to be made at the next SIGCHI workshop which was to be held 1987 in Toronto, Canada. No reference model was brought forward there either and the topic of a reference model seems to completely fade away as the focus of the domain of software engineering in user interface development then begins to shift towards the technical realization and implementation of user interfaces with attention gradually increasing on the topic of model driven development in the domain of user interface development. The concept of model driven development in the domain of user interface development to this day is one of the most intensely researched subfields, spawning its own workshop in the "Model Driven Development of Advanced User Interfaces" and generating great amounts of papers and articles (for examples see [CHI10], [MMJS09], [Stö10], [MK09], [PS97], [PEGM94], or [PE99]).

3.2 Models in the Domain of Software Engineering for the User Interface Development

"The goal of specification-based, or model-based approach, for user interface development is to propose a set of abstractions, development processes and tools enabling a engineering approach of user interface development. The characteristics of an engineering approach are its systematic (development based of rational principles), its reproducibility, its orientation towards quality criteria." [Lim04].

The keyword here being the *engineering approach*, which Limbourg goes on to characterize by its "systematic (development based of rational principles), its reproducibility". Contrasting that against what Knuth says about programming as an art (rather than a science), that "science is knowledge which we understand so well that we can teach it to a computer; and if we don't fully understand something, it is an art to deal with it." [Knu74], (a quotation that will reappear in section 4.1) it becomes immediately clear that the systematic and reproducible part of interface development subsequently can - from a software engineering point of view - only be that part which fully lies in the technical realm, the implementation of user interface development. How would a software engineer

---

[2] A concept that was also prevalent in the "User Interface Management Systems" debate at around the same time.

go about systematically reproducing the creativity needed for great, beautiful user interfaces? The obvious answer is, he can not and all effort from the software engineering domain in user interface development then must be focused on (i.e. *reduced to*) that part of user interface development in the domain of software engineering that *can* be grasped by just stipulated goals.

Keeping that in mind, Limbourg [Lim04] presents a total of three approaches in the domain of user interface development, based on the Diane methodology by Barthet [Bar88]. According to Limbourg the starting points for those three approaches are:

1. The internal view – relates to the UI implementation and its description as it is relevant for the UI developer.

2. The external view – relates to the interface appearance and its behavior, as perceived by the end user.

3. The conceptual view – provides an insight on the logical structure underlying a UI in designer's terms. A conceptual view provides the designer with a set of abstract concepts facilitating reasoning on the artifact that is being built (e.g., a finite state machine, a class diagram).

Limbourg then goes on to describe the different combinations of approaches possible from these three starting points, i.e. the internal-external generation approach, internal-conceptual derivation approach, conceptual-external, etc.

The interesting aspect here to note is that all three approaches focus on the technical realization of the software system, which in one case is being reached by creating a mock-up first which is then being implemented, in the second case by starting to implement right away and fitting a user-interface "on top" of the system, or in the last case by creating a model of the interface first, which can then be transformed (as much as possible: automatically) into a working user interface. The advantages of the last approach are clear: creating a model allows for the abstract description (or even definition, specification) of a user interface while remaining abstract and technology independent.

The first and second approach are not relevant to the concept of this thesis so will not be inspected. The third approach is the one of relevance here and the question that is being posed is: which then are the models and methodologies available for the model driven approach? The following are a representative collection of such.

3.3 Models and Methodologies for the MDD Approach in UI Development

Inspecting the models and methodologies available for user interface development in the domain of software engineering it becomes clear, that software engineering as a discipline very much perceives the user interface as an aspect that falls into its own area of responsibility. This perspective is perfectly comprehensible, given the fact that the user interface in a software system consists of software itself, and thus must be part of the entire development process[3]. It must then, however, be inspected to what extent the contemporary models and methodologies in the domain of software engineering, especially those for user interface development, take the aspects of interactivity, of usability into account and, subsequently, reflect them appropriately.

This section starts with the representation and brief overview of three predominant and influential models and tools in the domain of software engineering:

- the Model-View-Controller (MVC) model – a model for the structural technical implementation of object oriented software systems

- the Unified Modeling Language (UML)[4] – a model for the description of technical systems, i.e. software systems

- the Reference Model of Open Distributed Processing (RM-ODP) – a model for the provision of a standardized and clearly defined vocabulary needed for the accurate modeling (i.e. description or specification) of open distributed systems

Inspecting these models and tools in regard to their consideration of user interface development aspects sheds some light on why the aspect of usability in the domain of software engineering has historically received such little attention.

After the inspection of those three models, the presentation of other contemporary models and methodologies in the domain of software engineering for user interface development follows.

---
[3] More on that thought in section 2.3.
[4] While strictly speaking the UML is a graphical modeling language itself, it is based on a model, namely, the meta-model of the UML and produces models in the diagrams produced with it. In this chapter the focus lies on that underlying structure of the UML as a model and the models produced with it.

3.3.1 Model View Controller

The Model View Controller (MVC) paradigm is an architectural design pattern used in software engineering [Mös93] and is underlying about every relevant contemporary software development framework (prominent examples include Microsoft's .NET framework for application development, Microsoft's ASP.NET framework for website-based application development, Apple's Cocoa framework for application development, Apple's iOS framework for mobile app development, Palm's Mojo framework for mobile app development, or the prevalent combination of PHP / HTML / CSS in website development).

First described by Trygve Reenskaug in 1979 during his stay at Xerox PARC the MVC paradigm was initially conceived as a "general solution to the problem of users controlling a large and complex data set" [Ree10] in user interfaces implemented in Smalltalk. The concept of the MVC paradigm is the conceptual separation of the objects of an object oriented system into three parts, namely the model, the view, and the controller.

With the model being responsible for the data an application works on, the view being responsible for the representation of data to the user, and the controller holding the business logic for working on the data according to the directives received from the view (effectively, the user). Each object should clearly fall into one of these three groups and thus be, either, a model, controller, or view object. A system that adheres to the MVC paradigm would then allow the same model to be used on different platforms, with only the controller and view having to be adjusted to the different environment of another platform.

Figure 3.1 depicts the underlying concept of the MVC paradigm in which direct associations are represented by solid lines, indirect association, i.e. via an observer, by dashed lines. In the following

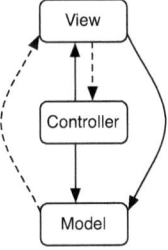

Figure 3.1: Model-View-Controller Concept

a brief overview of the three components of the MVC paradigm are given.

Model

The model encapsulates the data and basic behavior. Model objects contain business logic and special knowledge. In a well-designed MVC application any data that is part of the persistent state of the application should reside in the model objects once the application has loaded its data. Because model objects contain knowledge related to a specific problem domain, model objects tend to be highly reusable.

The most important aspect to observe is that the model is to be completely independent of the presentation and controlling of the user interface. In the concept of MVC then, the model receives information about changes to be made to the data from the controller, while the view may only observe the model and can then react to changes in the data accordingly, i.e. by updating the presentation of values in the user interface.

Controller

The controller is responsible for translating the user interactions with the view into actions to be performed by the model, i.e. on the data. By interpreting the outcome of the model actions it responds to the user interactions by selecting the appropriate view.

View

The view is responsible for presenting the required data from the model to the user and handles the user-interaction. The view contains its own controlling and is aware of the data contained in the model (read-only access), however, it is not the view's responsibility to process the data received from the user.

MVC and Interaction Aspects of the System

The Model-View-Controller paradigm is a good example of a model in the domain of software engineering of the technical structure of a software system. Its architectural design concept is an engineering driven design pattern from the early days of the object oriented paradigm. By adhering to the MVC design pattern the reusability of classes, especially the objects of the "model" (from

State of the Art CHAPTER 3

the MVC perspective) is greatly increased, the structure of the code becomes less entangled and interdependent which in turn allows for a higher grade of maintainability and extensibility. Basing an application design on the MVC architectural design pattern does not, however, address or even answer in any way the aspects of usability and user interaction sufficiently, as these aspects are not what MVC is concerned with.

While the MVC architectural design pattern describes a clear structuring and policy of separation of concern in the object structure of an application, i.e. on the technical level of the application, it does not include any aspects regarding *how* the user interacts with the application from the perspective of whichever possibilities would be available. It is a purely implementation oriented paradigm which focuses entirely on the internal services and functionality of an application.

But the design decisions regarding the way the user is to interact with the application are obviously of fundamental importance to designing an application in a way perceived as "user friendly" and with good usability. To allow for such a discourse to take place, then, a theoretical environment, i.e. a model, must be created that provokes and furthers the leading to a position where decisions relevant to the usability of an application will be made. Once this process has taken place, MVC can then provide the general architecture the objects need to be implemented for.

In order to establish a theoretical environment supportive of a discourse about interaction specific aspects a model is needed that addresses these interaction specific aspects by providing a mental lense on the structural interdependencies of interaction specific aspects. Again, MVC does not provide this as it was never intended to.

3.3.2 Unified Modeling Language

The Unified Modeling Language is a good example of a model in the domain of software engineering and the expressive needs required to describe the technical aspects of a software system. In its current version 2.3 UML is a standardized general-purpose graphical modeling language for the field of software engineering comprising fourteen different diagram types for describing software-intensive systems. UML was created and is being maintained by the Object Management Group (OMG). Figure 3.2 provides an overview of the diagram types as a UML class diagram, with the leaf-classes being the actual diagram types and the classes named in *italicized* font being abstract, i.e. non-instantiable, superclasses. This means, that while the Profile, Class, Composite Structure,

Component, Deployment, Object, and Package Diagram are all *Structure Diagrams*, there is actually no Structure Diagram itself.

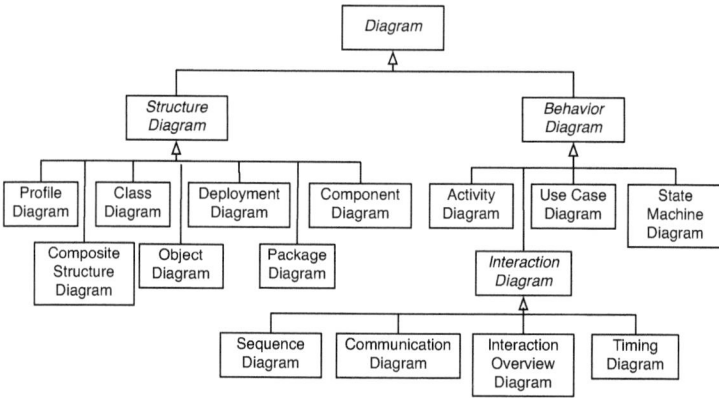

Figure 3.2: The fourteen diagram types of UML 2.3 represented by a UML class diagram.

A Quick Overview of the UML 2.2 Diagrams

It is neither in the scope nor the interest of this work to elaborate on the UML diagram types but in order to illustrate the nature and purpose of UML and thus pointing out certain shortcomings in regard to the domain of user interface design and development a quick overview of the diagram types is needed and hence given here.

Profile Diagram

The profile diagram is for modeling on the meta-model level, showing stereotypes as classes and profiles as packages. It is useful for extending and modifying UML to specific needs.

Class Diagram

The class diagram shows the structure of the system to be modeled. It shows the essential static properties as well as their relation to one another. The class diagram addresses the question of the structure of the modeled system's data and behavior.

Composite Structure Diagram

The composite structure diagram allows the modeling of the internal structure of a class, component, or use case, including the interaction points for collaboration between these classifiers.

Component Diagram

The component diagram is used for modeling how a system is split up into components. The components, their interrelationships, interactions, and public interfaces are depicted.

Object Diagram

The object diagram provides a snapshot of a system at a specific time during runtime. This diagram type shows class instances (objects), components, nodes, associations, and attributes.

Package Diagram

The package diagram shows the structuring of the system into distinct groups and their relationships and dependencies. By bundling model elements into packages higher levels of abstraction can be achieved in the model.

Activity Diagram

Activity diagrams are used for modeling the overall flow of control in the system. It depicts high-level business processes, including data flow, and operational step-by-step workflows.

Use Case Diagram

Use case diagrams are used for modeling the functionality provided by the system to the users, which are modeled as actors. The goals of the actors are represented by use cases.

State Machine Diagram

State machine diagrams provide a standardized notation to describe the states an object or interaction may be in, as well as the transition between states.

Sequence Diagram

Sequence diagrams depict the communication between objects as a sequence of exchanged messages. These diagrams are also used to indicate the lifespan of the communicating objects in relation to the messages sent and received.

Communication Diagram

The communication diagram is a hybrid by modeling static structure of a system as well as its dynamic behavior. It depicts instances of classes, their interrelationships, and the message flow between them.

Interaction Overview Diagram

Interaction overview diagrams provide the means to modeling the interaction of a system from a higher abstraction by depicting interaction diagrams as nodes in this diagram type. This then allows for the nesting of complex interactions within this diagram type without confusing cluttering.

Timing Diagram

Timing diagrams are used when the time of messages received and sent is of crucial importance to the modeling of the system.

UML and Interaction Aspects of the System

UML is the de facto industry standard modeling language for modeling, i.e. describing software systems. With its wide range of diagram types about every relevant technical aspect of a system can be modeled.

To consider the prevalence of UML in the domain of software engineering it is striking to realize that there is no means to model usability related aspects of a software system, for example the modality in which an information transfer between the user and the system takes place. This tellingly illustrates the priority the usability of software systems has been given throughout the emergence of the domain of software engineering.

3.3.3 RM-ODP

The Reference Model for Open Distributed Processing (RM-ODP) is an industry standard for modeling open, distributed systems and has been created by the International Organization for Standardization (ISO), the International Electrotechnical Commission (IEC), and the Telecommunication Standardization Sector (ITU-T). It is also known under ITU-T Rec. X.901-X.904 and ISO/IEC 10746. Its architecture separates five distinctly different viewpoints on a system which all build on top of the RM-ODP foundation, a collection of model elements of most fundamental nature to any modeling activity. According to the specification of RM-ODP itself,

> a viewpoint (on a system) is an abstraction that yields a specification of the whole system related to a particular set of concerns. [RO98]

RM-ODP comprises five non-hierarchical viewpoints:

- Enterprise viewpoint - which is concerned with the purpose, scope and policies governing the activities of the specified system within the organization of which it is a part

- Information viewpoint - which is concerned with the kinds of information handled by the system and constraints on the use and interpretation of that information

- Engineering viewpoint - which is concerned with the infrastructure required to support system distribution

- Computational viewpoint - which is concerned with the functional decomposition of the system into a set of objects that interact at interfaces - enabling system distribution

- Technology viewpoint - which is concerned with the choice of technology to support system distribution

Each viewpoint is being represented in the RM-ODP specification by a viewpoint language, which allows to express a specification of the system from that particular viewpoint. Due to the object modeling concepts each viewpoint adheres to it is then possible to identify relationships between the different viewpoint specifications and to assert correspondences between the representations of the system in different viewpoints.

RM-ODP and Interaction Aspects of the System

RM-ODP is an incredibly powerful and encompassing model for the description of open distributed systems, however, it does not provide any useful means for the modeling of the interaction related aspects of a system, as this is not at all the focus or even intention of RM-ODP.

RM-ODP as the Foundation for RM-IOS

The realized concept of a model providing several viewpoints on a system, however, is a potent one which has inspired the very structure of the Reference Model for Interaction Oriented Systems introduced in this thesis. This concept will be seized during the development approach of the model created in this thesis (see chapter 4).

Additionally, RM-ODP represents a particularly solid model structure, grounded in the RM-ODP foundation, a collection of model elements relevant and useful to *any* kind of modeling. In order to provide the model developed in this thesis with a sound foundation it will be built on top of the RM-ODP foundation, effectively taking advantage of the profound expertise, knowledge, and experience present in the RM-ODP and its foundation. This architectural decision provides a solid architectural basis for the model elements then introduced in the model of this thesis.

3.3.4 UsiXML

"UsiXML (which stands for USer Interface eXtensible Markup Language) is an XML-compliant markup language that describes the UI for multiple contexts of use such as Character User Interfaces (CUIs), Graphical User Interfaces (GUIs), Auditory User Interfaces, and Multimodal User Interfaces" is the definition of UsiXML given on the UsiXML's consortium's website [usi07]. UsiXML is situated in the domain of multi-path UI development, which tries to bridge the gap between UI modeling and design of multi-platform UIs from the domain of HCI and program transformation from the domain of SE.

UsiXML's main focus lies on the description of UIs by providing a multi-layered concept of UI abstraction which allows for the description of multi-platform, multi-context UIs. The four layers are:

- Task & Concept
- Abstract User Interface

State of the Art   CHAPTER 3

- Concrete User Interface
- Final User Interface

For the realization of this concept "UsiXML relies on a transformational approach that progressively moves from the Task and Concept level to the FUI" [Sta08] (additionally see [LV04] and [Van07]). UsiXML as a model focuses on the realization of provision of user interfaces independent of the technical realization and is strongly anchored in the model driven development paradigm and the model transformation school of thought. The purpose of UsiXML is not to model a system from different perspectives or offer the mental tools needed for the fundamental interaction related aspects of a system.

3.3.5 UMLi

UMLi is a minimal extension of the UML "used for the integrated design of applications an their user interfaces" [SP00]. The concept behind UMLi is that most model-based user interface development environments (MB-UIDE) provide means for modeling the data over which the interface acts, but "provide limited facilities for describing the functionality of the application for which the interface is being constructed" [SP03]. This weakness in application modeling of MB-UIDEs is the main domain of UML. UMLi's user interface diagram provides these additional elements to the UML:

- FreeContainers
- Containers
- Inputters
- Editors
- Displayers
- ActionInvokers

However, the scope of UMLi is restricted to form-based user interfaces which are particularly prevalent in websites. UMLi does not provide means to model fundamental aspects of usability such as the modality or the perceivability of a system's user interface elements.

3.3.6 GOMS

GOMS stands for "Goals", "Operators", "Methods", and "Selection Rules" and is a model for a leveled analysis proposed by theorists from the Carnegie-Mellon University [CNM83] [JK96]. It falls into the category of task models for task analysis. While GOMS is not a model necessarily situated in the domain of software engineering for user interface development it is still relevant here as it well represents the domain of task models in the discipline of cognitive psychology related to user interface development.

The core idea behind GOMS is to decompose a user's actions into small, measurable steps. The reasoning behind this idea is the concept of the user firstly formulating certain goals and subgoals she wishes to achieve, i.e. editing a document (goal) or inserting a word (subgoal). The next cognitive process then is the user thinking in terms of operators, which are "elementary perceptual, motor, or cognitive acts, whose execution is necessary to change any aspect of the user's mental state or to affect the task environment" [CNM83, p. 144], such as "press up-arrow key, move hand to mouse, etc.". The user then decides on how she will reach her goal, which is represented by the selection rules, i.e. deciding to pressing CTRL+P to print or, alternatively, clicking on the icon showing a small printer.

While GOMS provides valuable information for the analysis of how a user interacts with a system, it provides virtually no help during the conception, modeling, and design of an interactive system.

3.4 Dialog Models

In [Lim04] an exhaustive collection of dialog models is listed and examined from the (semi-)automatic model-code transformation perspective. The following is a recapitulation of those relevant to the domain of dialog modeling but from the perspective of interdisciplinary, holistic modeling in the domain of user interface development.

3.4.1 Backus-Naur Form (BNF) grammars

The Backus-Naur Form is a technique to express context-free grammars. It is useful for describing the structure of documents, the syntax of programming languages, or communication protocols. While this approach is highly useful for the formal description of structures, e.g. command-structures, documents-structures, Limbourg summarizes correctly when he says that "grammars are effective

```
<telephone-number> := +<country-code><area-code><line-number>
```

Figure 3.3: Example of Backus-Naur-Form

for expressing sequential commands or users actions but when it comes to multimodal or direct manipulation they tend to be heavy to manipulate" [Lim04, page 44]. Additionally it is overly apparent that the BNF stems from a purely technical, formal approach to the description of systems. Being a low-level model it is does not provide the means to describe a system from a high-level, abstract point of view, i.e. inclusive of the interaction relevant aspects such as multimodality, user's perceptibility of system elements, and so forth.

3.4.2 State Transition Diagrams

A state transition diagram is a graphical representation of an automaton with finite states and its behavior, represented by states and the transitions connecting those states. A prevalent model in the computer-science subfield of system-theory, state transition diagrams it is helpful for visualizing complex systems and their behavior. The UML provides a "state diagram" to model state transition diagrams.

Connecting state transition diagrams with the domain of UI development, Shneiderman proposes the reduction of state transition diagrams to window managers in graphical state transition diagrams [SP05].

3.4.3 Statecharts

Akin to state transition diagrams, statecharts are another way to model the dynamic behavior of a system. The UML (see above) offers the statechart-diagram as one of its diagram types. State charts provide the means to model the state a system can be in and the possible transitions to another state the system can then be changed into by fulfilling the triggering event requirement.

Some of the advantages of statecharts are the possibilities to include restrictions and conditions on the state-changing events, the nesting of subsystems into systems, and the offering of a way to model external interrupts on states.

State of the Art CHAPTER 3

Statecharts are, however, not suitable for the abstract and general description of a system and its interaction but are instead a way to describe the internal changes of the system's state, which obviously requires (or leads to) a complete conception of the states of a system. Additionally the aspect of the styling of a system is not part of a statechart diagram and statecharts themselves offer no extension-point for that.

3.4.4 Petri Nets

Petri Nets are a mathematical model for modeling concurrent systems. They are completely formalized which makes them ideal for the modeling of technical systems, i.e. systems that are to be implemented in a programming language. Petri Nets diagrams show a bipartite, directed graph consisting of places (states), and transitions (state-changing operators). Transitions can be specified to fire (be triggered) under the condition of a certain amount of tokens arriving in the preceding state which is a powerful tool when modeling conditional concurrency and checking for dead-ends in a system, i.e. states, which the system can not recover from.

Petri Nets are originally not at all meant for UI modeling, however Palanque offers an interesting approach to utilizing Petri Nets for UI modeling in [Pal94].

3.5 ISO Standards Relevant to UI Development

Several ISO standards exist about aspects relevant to the domain of UI development. The ones that seemed most notable to the author in regard to this thesis are briefly introduced here.

3.5.1 ISO 13407

The ISO 13407:1999 titled "Human-centered design processes for interactive systems" is a norm describing a user centered software development methodology. ISO 13407 outlines four essential activities in a user-centered design project:

- Requirements gathering - Understanding and specifying the context of use

- Requirements specification - Specifying the user and organizational requirements

- Design - Producing designs and prototypes

- Evaluation - Carrying out user-based assessment of the site

The focus of this norm lies on the methodology, i.e. the approach to the development of user interfaces and does not provide a structural model for actually modeling the system.

3.5.2 ISO 9241

ISO 9241, titled "Ergonomics of Human System Interaction", is a standard consisting of multiple parts. It describes requirements to the work-environment, hard- and software and aims to help in avoiding hazards to the health. It is divided into 9 substandards numbered in increments of 100:

- 100 series - Software ergonomics
- 200 series - Human system interaction processes
- 300 series - Displays and display related hardware
- 400 series - Physical input devices - ergonomics principles
- 500 series - Workplace ergonomics
- 600 series - Environment ergonomics
- 700 series - Application domains - Control rooms
- 900 series - Tactile and haptic interactions

This standard provides a normative description of those areas listed above. Its focus lies on the circumstantial conditions commonly confronted with in those fields.

3.5.3 ISO 9126

Not so much a norm about usability of software per se, but actually a norm about the assessment of the overall quality of software, of which usability is one of the aspects. This norm, titled "Software engineering — Product quality", is divided into four parts, and provides an evaluative description of a software system's quality attributes. The four parts are:

- Quality Model

State of the Art CHAPTER 3

- External Metrics
- Internal Metrics
- Quality in Use Metrics

The norm lists several aspects of software systems characteristic to the quality of the software system. These characteristics are:

- Functionality
- Reliability
- Usability
- Efficiency
- Maintainability
- Portability

The aspects of usability are concerned with the aspects of a system's understandability, learnability, operability, attractiveness, and usability compliance.
ISO 9126 has been superseded by ISO 25000 since 2005.

3.5.4 ISO 25000

The ISO organization states that "ISO/IEC 25000:2005 provides guidance for the use of the new series of International Standards named Software product Quality Requirements and Evaluation (SQuaRE)."
It provides:

- Terms and definitions,
- Reference models,
- General guide,
- Individual division guides, and

- Standards for requirements specification, planning and management, measurement and evaluation purposes.

The reference models of ISO 25000 are normative reference models describing the interdependencies between the process quality, the internal quality attributes, the external quality attributes, and the quality in use attributes. They are not descriptive reference models of the structural composition of a system from different perspectives defined by different areas of skill and responsibility.

3.6 Conclusion

This chapter exhibited a collection of models and methodologies currently prevalent in the domain of software engineering for user interface development. The models and methodologies selected to be presented here serve two purposes: One, to point out the model background in the domain of software engineering in general - as this discipline does set a strong claim on the discipline of user interface development - and thereby to demonstrate the very technical and implementation driven nature of those models. Two, to point towards models and methodologies relevant and related to the field of work done in this thesis.

It showed that several models and methodologies exist that try to answer the challenges posed by the domain of user interface development and each model and methodology offers a unique contribution to this field; however, an interdisciplinary descriptive reference model that provides a multiple perspective based approach, including the different disciplines integral to the domain of user interface development does currently not exist.

Chapter 4

Development and Overview of the RM-IOS

This chapter presents the analytical development process that led to the perspective based Reference Model for Interaction Oriented Systems that has been developed in an attempt to fulfill the concepts formulated in the hypothesis (see section 1.2).

The chapter begins with exposing the motivation that initiated this project which serves two purposes:

1. To raise awareness for the problems that the model addresses and tries to answer to.

2. To describe the problem and solution domain of the model in order to introduce the reader to the underlying thoughts that drove the creation of the model.

Section 4.2 then describes the development process of the model, portraying the analytical thought process underlying the creation of the Reference Model for Interaction Oriented Systems.

Section 4.3 provides a description of the final model, to make the actual model more accessible to the reader. For the same purpose section 5.6 offers a graphical overview of the model in form of UML class diagrams, as mentioned below.

The chapter concludes with section 4.4 which answers six questions of defining quality for any model. The answers to these six questions can be understood as the "meta-structure" of the model.

4.1 Motivation

The domain of user interface engineering and "good usability" today is still something that is viewed mostly to be a matter of art rather than science. Donald E. Knuth aptly writes

> Science is knowledge which we understand so well that we can teach it to a computer; and if we don't fully understand something, it is an art to deal with it. [Knu74]"

about the difference between art and science[1].

Taking a look at the recommendations of established opinions on the conception, design, and realization of user interfaces one inevitably comes to the conclusion, that user interface development must (still) be considered a matter of art rather than a matter of science. Of course this conclusion does not deny those aspects of user interface development of their scientific nature when they are, in fact, scientific. But as Shneiderman for example states in his "golden rules" that the user interface is to be designed in such a way that it "support(s) internal locust of control" or that it "offer(s) informative feedback". Examining the guides and recommendations for good user interface design given by the commonly accepted experts in this field, such as Shneiderman, Cooper, Raskin, Buxton, Nielsen, it becomes obvious how difficult it is to frame these aspects scientifically. As while all of these recommendations are undeniably important aspects of what should be perceived as a good user interface it is nigh impossible to formally express them or even automatically check for them.

However, some aspects of user interface development are very well based firmly in science, especially those aspects with a background in cognitive psychology. As the knowledge of the human capacities in terms of perception and cognition, i.e. the human abilities and limits, are - where ascertained - the immovable fundament to be considered in the design and engineering of user interfaces.

To then separate those aspects of user interface development that can safely be considered "science" and, for now, leave those aspects that still must be considered "art" to the individual expert of the respective domain seems a worthy goal pursuing and is one of the goals of creating the Reference Model for Interaction Oriented Systems in this thesis.

Another defining characteristic of the domain of user interface development is its strong interdisciplinary nature, finding its roots in the fields of operating systems, human factors, systems integration, computer graphics, cognitive psychology, artificial intelligence, application programming, and

---

[1] In that paper he then goes on to illustrate that for that very same reason he believes programming to be a matter of art, rather than science. And despite the advances in programming languages, development techniques, frameworks, and methodologies over the past 36 years, the reasons for his argument still hold true today.

recently more and more in the field of art design, especially graphical design. It is then correct to deduce that successful user interface development, i.e. a process or methodology that produces in its conclusion a thoroughly satisfying user experience, involves several domains of skill and expertise. In order to allow domain transcending collaboration and imperatively preceding: domain transcending communication a common vocabulary must be provided so that experts with a background in different domains of skill may insert their expertise into the process of user interface development. Providing such a common vocabulary is another fundamentally important aspect that should be provided by a Reference Model for Interaction Oriented Systems.

Akin to just illustrated point of a common vocabulary is the establishing of a policy of separation of concern based on the skill and expertise coming together in the process of user interface development. A successful realization of such a policy of separation of concern would enable experts from different fields to be able to freely work with the aspects of their area of responsibility while resting assured that their decisions will not collide with decisions made by those working in other areas of responsibilities. In order to achieve the goal of establishing such a policy of separation of concern, the contact points for the different domains of skill and expertise must be affixed, effectively providing a vocabulary for the interface between the different domains of skill and expertise.

4.2 Development of the Model

After the preceding section has described the motivation of this model this section now describes the conceptual work that has led to the actual creation of the model.

As outlined in the introduction (see 1.3), the approach to creating a model that meets the expectations formulated in the hypothesis has to be a rational, analytical one, as the creation of such a model can not be achieved by calculations. Also the reiterative model construction of "modeling and testing" is a method not feasible during this thesis, as real testing would demand the collection of empirical data, which in turn would require the completion of several "real world" software projects in which RM-IOS is being used. This, however, stands contrary to the intention of the author to provide a model helpful to the current need of development tools in the field of user interface development.

However, the case study offered in chapter 6 does provide a proof of concept by examining a tiny example of how the RM-IOS can perform when actually applied in a practical context.

In the following now the rational, analytical approach taken to construct the RM-IOS will be described in a goal oriented manner, with the goal obviously being the creation of the Reference Model for Interaction Oriented Systems.

4.2.1 Towards a Reference Model for Interaction Oriented Systems

In the attempt of designing and creating a user interface to an application that provides state-of-the-art usability, several guidelines and suggestions exist, what aspects should be considered, how a user interface should behave, and how to approach the development of user interfaces (see [SP05] [CRC07] [Ras94] [Ras07] [Bux07] [Win96] [Gal07], and, although not focused on computer interfaces but human interaction with objects in general also [Nor90]).

But while a reference model such as aimed for here should not provide general advice regarding the methodology of user interface development, the experience and knowledge contained in the suggestions of those experts of user interface design and development offers valuable insight and inspiration regarding what model elements a reference must include to be of any real use. Furthermore, those suggestions can be inspected regarding the necessary expertise required during the user interface development process. All that has just been said is reason to examine the guidelines and suggestions by the user interface experts and use them as a starting point for the construction of a Reference Model for Interaction Oriented Systems.

The - in the opinion of the author - most concise suggestions regarding good user interface design can be found in Shneiderman's widely acknowledged and encompassing book "Designing the User Interface" [SP05]. In which he offers what he calls "eight golden rules of interface design" [SP05, 74-75] to guide designers and developers in their decisions about the user interface. Those eight golden rules are listed here in a summarized form.

Shneiderman's Eight Golden Rules of Interface Design

1. *Strive for consistency*
   Consistent sequences of actions should be required in similar situations; identical terminology should be used in prompts, menus, and help screens; and consistent commands should be employed throughout.

2. *Cater to universal usability*
Different users have different expectations and demands from the system they are using. Especially advanced users desire shortcuts for frequently used actions to speed up and slim down their workflows.

3. *Offer informative feedback*
Every action by the user should evoke feedback from the system. Feedback should be adequate to the importance or frequency of the action performed by the user.

4. *Design dialogs to yield closure*
Clearly indicating when a workflow is beginning, in the process, and ending is important information for the user to know. When a user finishes a certain workflow the system should inform about this in a clear way.

5. *Prevent errors*
Limit the user to input actually valid for the current state of the workflow and handle errors done by the user in a gracious and forgiving manner.

6. *Permit easy reversal of actions*
Actions by the user should be reversible which eases the stress caused by fear of failure and makes room for the user to freely explore the user interface.

7. *Support internal locus of control*
Design the system in a way that it is responsive to the user's input rather than making the user feel as if he's the one responding to - especially unexpected action by - the system.

8. *Reduce short-term memory load*
The human short-term memory is very limited (to approximately $7 +/- 2$ data chunks) and should not have to be filled with information the system could handle instead.

Shneiderman himself states that "these underlying principles must be interpreted, refined, and extended for each environment [...]" as they do not provide directly measurable values. And indeed there is no way to easily and reliably check a system for compliance with these rules. Some of the principles represented by each rule, however, can be captured in a single expression, i.e. rule # 6 can be captured in the expression "undo ability". Also, rule #1, #2, #3, and #5 can be similarly compressed which will be done further down.

Furthermore it is interesting to note, that Shneiderman does not refer to any styling aspects of the user interface, which could mislead to the assumption, that the styling of the user interface is irrelevant in the domain of usability. The correct conclusion, however, that can be drawn here is that the aspect of interface styling must obviously be independent of the interaction related aspects between the user and the system.

This reinforces the assumption, that a policy of separation of concern realized in the aimed for reference model should account for interaction related aspects belonging to a different area of expertise than styling aspects. The structure of the reference model will have to reflect this.

Returning to the "eight golden rules", extracting the key aspects from those five rules mentioned above a list like the following can be composed:

- *Terminology* - Rule #1 recommends uniform terminology and actions throughout the system.

- *Shortcuts* - Rule #2 recommends offering shortcuts to experienced users.

- *Feedback* - Rule #3 recommends to offer feedback to the user on every action.

- *Error Handling* - Rule #5 recommends a gracious and forgiving way to handle errors that can occur during the user interacting with the system. However, it must be differentiated between errors caused by some malfunction of the system, for example the lack of a mandatory network connection, lack of memory, and so forth, and "errors" caused by "false" input provided by the user. In this thesis an error and subsequently error handling will be understood as the failure of the system itself, bar any user input or handling. Any sort of input providable by the user, however nonsensical, shall be viewed simply as input. This distinction is important when the aspect of error handling later is not being allocated to the interaction related aspects but the functionality related aspects, as error handling in the way Shneiderman lists will be part of the system simply responding to user provided input.

- *Undo ability* - Rule #6 recommends enabling an easy reversal of actions to the user. While the ability to undo an unwanted action is a fundamental aspect of good usability design, this aspect can be viewed from two perspectives. The one perspective, where the user triggers the undo action. This would simply be an input that the system responds to accordingly, by providing the output of a previous system state. The other perspective, where the implementation of this provided undo functionality is a matter of system state- and memory management. In the former case the undo ability is simply viewed as a pair of input/output, in the latter case it is viewed as something in the realm of software development and memory management. This explains, why the undo ability as an aspect later on is not allocated to the interaction related aspects, but to the functionality related aspects.

Rule #4, #7, and #8 describe rather systemic aspects of the system which can not easily be represented in a single term.

Collecting Relevant Aspects

Additionally, the following aspects are obviously part of contemporary, interaction oriented systems and can be added to the collection. This list of aspects does not aim nor claim to be an all encompassing collection of aspects but it does provide an agreeable basis for further thinking about a structure underlying such a system in terms of different responsibilities and expertise required.

- *Security* - Making sure that information is secure from unauthorized access.
- *Search* - Enabling the user to perform sundry search operations on the system's data.
- *Data Handling & Storage* - The system is working on data and needs to store data appropriately.
- *Data Input / Data Output* - Data is being provided to the system by the user and the user expects data output from the system.
- *Networking* - Many modern systems perform some sort of networking operations.
- *Technical Requirements* - Every system relies on certain technical requirements to be met in order to function properly. Also, the state of the art in hardware sets the frame in which interaction solutions can be devised.
- *Response Time* - For some time critical systems response time, i.e. the time the system needs to respond to some event, can be an important factor.
- *Input / Output* - The input from the user to the system needs to be provided by the user in a certain way as the output from the system to the user needs to be offered in a certain way.
- *Modality* - Modern systems often take advantage of several modalities to communicate with the user effectively.

- *Accessibility* - The elements a user needs for interacting with the system need to be easily accessible. Spatially, in matters of hardware elements, in matters of software elements rather a combination of spatial aspects and "numbers of clicks needed".
- *Terminology* - The elements of a user interface are named to implicate the action that can be performed. Overly technical terminology can confuse the user without technical knowledge.
- *Appearance* - The user interface of a system has a certain appearance, whether that be a visual, aural, or haptic appearance.
- *Typeface* - The text in a visual user interface is set in a certain typeface.
- *Color* - The elements of a visual user interface are colored.
- *Iconography* - Icons play a vital part in the still prevalent WIMP (Window, Icon, Menu, Pointing Device) based interface and allow visual representation of certain actions.
- *Layout* - The elements of a visual or haptic user interface must be placed in the available space and in accordance with the principles of good accessibility.
- *Menu Architecture* - Menus are another important aspect in the WIMP based interface and need to be designed in a way that supports the user's typical workflows.

This list of items is presented graphically in figure 4.1 and represents a lose collection of aspects that are relevant during any software development process, subsequently must contain aspects relevant during the user interface development.

Structuring Relevant Aspects

As a next step towards filtering out those aspects relevant for the user interface development process and, at the same time, finding a structure supportive of the goal of constructing a perspective-based model, relations are drawn between those aspects that obviously have some sort of relationship to one another. These relationships are to be understood as an unqualified link, defined by the description provided below. That reasoning behind the relationships between the elements drawn in figure 4.2 are given in the following list:

- 1 *Security - Data Handling & Storage* - Security is realized by storing and handling the data in such a way that unauthorized access to the data is prevented.

Development and Overview of the RM-IOS CHAPTER 4

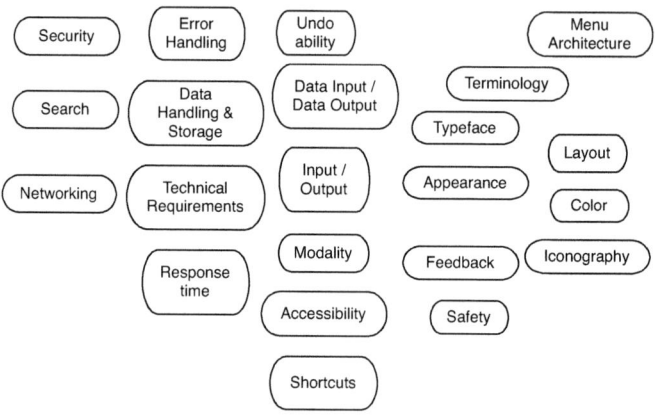

Figure 4.1: Aspects of a contemporary IOS

- 2 *Search - Data Handling & Storage* - A search function needs data to work on for the results to be returned.

- 3 *Networking - Data Handling & Storage* - Data is sent over the network and thus needs to be prepared and handled accordingly.

- 4 *Technical Requirements & Networking* - Every kind of networking capability requires according network devices to be present.

- 5 *Error Handling - Data Handling & Storage* - Preventing permanent loss of data by means of keeping several versions of the data worked on is a basic concept of handling errors caused by user maloperation.

- 6 *Technical Requirements - Data Handling & Storage* - Depending on the decisions how the data handling and storage is to be performed, different technical requirements arise.

- 7 *Technical Requirements - Response Time* - In systems with critical response time requirements the technical requirements must be considered accordingly.

- 8 *Undo Ability - Error Handling* - An undo ability often is a fundamental aspect of allowing users to handle their own faulty actions by simply restoring a previous state of the data.

- 9 *Undo Ability - Data Handling & Storage* - Easy reversal of actions to a previous state of the data worked on is commonly realized by an undo ability within the application.

- 10 *Data Input / Data Output - Data Handling & Storage* - Depending on the quantity and kind of data the system receives from the user and is to present to the user different ways of storing and handling the data will be considered.

- 11 *Technical Requirements - Input / Output* - Different ways of entering data require according interface devices to be present. Also the progress in hardware development enables different ways of interacting with a system.

- 12 *Input / Output - Modality* - The choice of modality has a fundamental impact on the way interaction can occur.

- 13 *Modality - Accessibility* - Multimodal interfaces help the user to access the system's functions and thus facilitate easier accessibility.

- 14 *Input / Output - Data Input / Data Output* - Depending on what kind of data input is to be provided by the user to the system and what kind of data output is to be presented by the system to the user different ways of how that data exchange is to happen will be considered.

- 15 *Accessibility - Safety* - Aspects of user-safety have to be considered when thinking about a system's accessibility.

- 16 *Accessibility - Shortcuts* - Shortcuts extend the accessibility of a system typically to advanced users.

- 17 *Input / Output - Feedback* - Feedback to the user on his actions can be presented in many different ways.

- 18 *Modality - Feedback* - Feedback can be given to the user through different modalities.

- 19 *Input / Output - Appearance* - The way the user interacts with the system through the interface devices can be styled in different ways without fundamentally changing the way the interaction is taking place.

- 20 *Appearance - Typeface* - The choice of typeface has a fundamental effect on the appearance of a visual, text-including user interface.

- 21 *Appearance - Layout* - The elements of the user interface must be arranged (in a layout) which in turn effects the appearance of the user interface.

- 22 *Appearance - Color* - Every visually present entity has a color, and the color of the elements in a user interface effect the appearance of the user interface.

- 23 *Appearance - Iconography* - The use of icons changes the appearance of a user interface.

- 24 *Layout - Menu Architecture* - Menus, their content and placement on the user interface are an integral part of the layout of the user interface.

- 25 *Appearance - Terminology* - A homogenous and consistent terminology gives the user interface a consistent appearance.

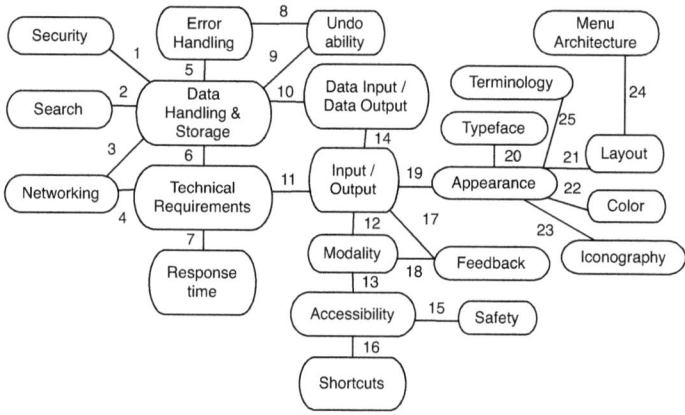

Figure 4.2: Aspects of a contemporary IOS and their relations

Grouping Relevant Aspects

Inspecting figure 4.2 it is now possible to identify clusters of aspects, that share a certain common affiliation: the blue colored aspects obviously share a common affiliation by all being concerned with the basic functionality, or "backbone", of a system. The green colored aspects obviously share a common affiliation by all being concenred with interaction related aspects of a system. And the yellow colored aspects obviously share a common affiliation by all being concerned with the aesthetic styling of a system.

Additionally it shows, that grouping those aspects thusly divides the entire collection of aspects into three sets of aspects, separated at points where few connecting links exist. This concurrence between the groups of aspects being defined (and hence separated from one another) by, both, commonality of their concerns and few connecting links again reinforces the initially made assumption that it is possible to support a policy of separation of concern within the model's structure by reflecting these groups and their boundaries of responsibilities accordingly[2].

By separating these groups of aspects at those links three important purposes are being served: firstly, these groups and the decisions that fall into their area of responsibility can be viewed independently from one another, i.e. deciding what data-structure or network protocol will be used has no interrelated connection with what background color the window will have. This means, that those aspects bundled in any of the three groups can be viewed and manipulated independently from one another, with the exception of those aspects, where a relationship exists into an aspect of another group. In this case the decisions made regarding one of the two linked aspects might very well effect the other and vice versa.

Secondly, the groups of aspects formed fall into a certain field of expertise which makes it possible to include the knowledge of specialists into the process of designing and developing a system by clearly defining areas of responsibilities.

Thirdly, it realizes the postulated requirement of "mirroring the separated domains of skill, knowledge, and expertise required to cope with the needs of successful interaction design and implementation" as formulated in the hypothesis (see 1.2) by a proposed policy of separation of concern, realized by the borders of the areas of responsibility articulated through the groups of aspects.

Figure 4.3 shows the colored collection of aspects to show the three groups.

---

[2]Obviously this fact leads to the three perspectives of functionality, interaction, and style the reference model for interaction oriented system implements. A characteristic of the model which in foresight seemed verisimilar, and in hindsight almost inevitable.

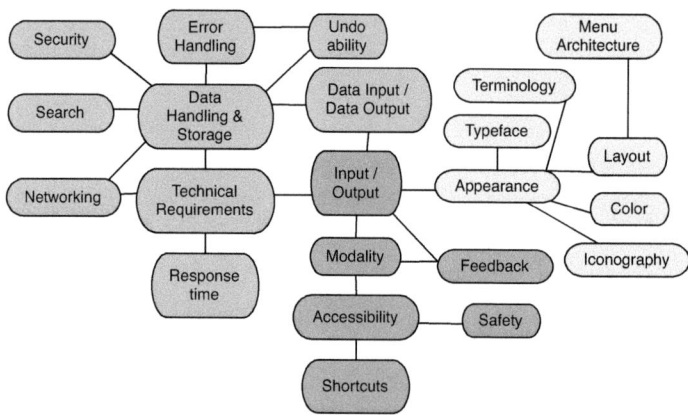

Figure 4.3: Aspects of a contemporary IOS grouped by colors - 1

Selecting Relevant Aspects

Inspecting these groups on figure 4.3 it is apparent that many of the aspects colored in blue (the aspects concerned with the internal aspects and functionality of the system) fall into the domain of conventional software engineering.

For the purpose of the creation of a Reference Model for Interaction Oriented Systems this is dispositive in two respects: firstly, it is not the author's intention for the reference model of interaction oriented systems to overlap with the well researched area of software engineering, and, secondly, these aspects have only remotely to do with the domain of user interface development. Following this line of thought it becomes obvious, that the elements in figure 4.3 that meet those criteria should be excluded from the conceptual process of creating a Reference Model for Interaction Oriented Systems.

The result of this selective process is depicted in figure 4.4, where those aspects falling into just described category are now marked by the hatched blue bubbles. The only remaining aspect is that of "Data Input / Data Output", which is concerned with what data is being provided to the system by the user as input and what data the user expects from the system as output. Also, the bubble containing the aspect of "Technical Requirements" is being excluded from the further process of creating a Reference Model for Interaction Oriented Systems. The reasoning for this decision is that while any kind of interaction is bound to a technical realization by providing respective devices for the interaction and the technical progress unlocks new means for human computer interaction, the technical state of the art is rather a given situation at any point in time and thus does not need to be included in a Reference Model for Interaction Oriented Systems. This is to say that the aspect of interface devices is simply a matter that is part of the overall thought process during the design and development of user interfaces.

The aspect of "Data Input / Data Output", however, describes the absolute essential core of a system's functionality and must also serve as the connecting link between:

- the aspects concerned with the internal realization of an interaction oriented system,
- the externally provided functionality of an interaction oriented system,
- and especially the interaction related aspects of an interaction oriented system.

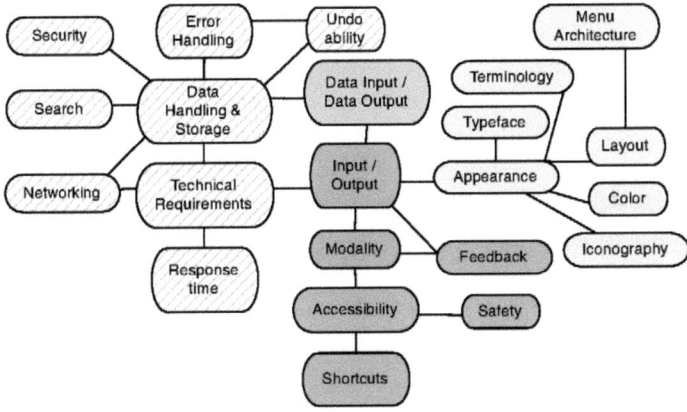

Figure 4.4: Aspects of a contemporary IOS grouped by colors - 2

Inspecting figure 4.4 the remaining (fully colored) aspects are now distinct clusters of three certain areas of expertise within the area of user interface development. These three areas of expertise can immediately be identified and labeled as:

1. the aspects concerned with the functionality of an interaction oriented system

2. the aspects concerned with the interaction between the user and the system, and

3. the aspects concerned with the styling of the system.

It follows that an interaction oriented system can be described to a satisfyingly complete degree when viewed and described from three perspectives. The perspectives of *functionality, interaction,* and *style*.

The Reference Model for Interaction Oriented Systems must reflect this and can realize this by drawing inspiration from the perspective based approach found in RM-ODP, where five perspectives on an open distributed system are provided[3].

Having arrived at this selection of aspects, separated into areas of expertise and responsibility the actual construction of the Reference Model for Interaction Oriented Systems can begin by critically inspecting those remaining aspects and considering how they can be appropriately reflected in a reference model.

Furthermore, considering the holistic nature of user interface development, certain aspects must be identified which are of influencing impact to the decisions made in more than one of the three areas of responsibility. This will be achieved by examining each element to be added to the model and answering the question "is the aspect this element addresses of influencing importance to more than one area of responsibility?". Should this question be answered positively, then that model element must be placed in a fourth group of elements, which will aptly be labeled the "foundation" of RM-IOS. This foundation will then include model elements which are of fundamental and defining importance to an interaction oriented system.

Also it must be possible to reference one specific interface element from each perspective, in order to enable the communication about interface elements across the three perspectives of functionality, interaction, and style[4]. The essential characteristic of the elements included in the Reference Model for Interaction Oriented Systems must be that of a timeless nature, i.e. meta aspects of any interaction oriented system. This is to say that while the actual way of interaction may change over the course of time, the fact that the end-user can be communicated with through his senses will not change. And while the actual interface elements may drastically change over time, the fact that any visual element occupies a certain amount of space will never change. These underlying

---

[3]In RM-ODP those perspectives are called *viewpoints* and are the enterprise viewpoint, computational viewpoint, technology viewpoint, engineering viewpoint, and information viewpoint. A more elaborate inspection of RM-ODP has been provided in section 3.3.3.

[4]This concept has been realized in the model element of the *interaction object*.

principles are what has just been labeled as the aspects of "timeless nature" and the reference model for interaction oriented system attempts to capture a meaningful amount of those.

Finally the reasoning behind every individual model element will be addressed in the explanations which are part of each model element description in section 5.1.

4.3 RM-IOS - Description

The section now provides a description of the four parts of the Reference Model for Interaction Oriented Systems. These descriptions are a summary of each of the four parts of the model and, together with the class diagrams of the model in section 5.6 offer a general overview of the Reference Model for Interaction Oriented Systems.

The model consists of four parts, namely, a foundation and three nonhierachical parts, each providing model elements for a specific perspectives one can have on an interaction oriented system. There is no explicit or implicit notion about the importance of the perspectives in comparison to one another nor does the model imply any kind of chronological order in which the three perspectives described by the model should be used.

The definition of elements in multiple perspectives is to be understood as additive to the definition of that element in the foundation. For example, the definition of the *interaction object* in the foundation encompasses those aspects, that are common to an interaction object in all three perspectives. The definition of the *interaction object* in the functionality perspective then extends that fundamental definition by adding aspects relevant to that particular perspective, in this case, aspects relevant when viewing an interaction object from a functionality point of view.

This technique, common to all technical, class based structures as, for example, object oriented programming languages, enables not only an iterative refinement of a concept from the imprecise general, down to the precise special, it also is the key to viewing one and the same object from different perspectives, i.e. exposing those aspects relevant to that perspective and fading out those aspects irrelevant to that perspective, effectively realizing a policy of separation of concern in the structure of the model.

Additionally, the propagation of the interaction object as an anchor element in all three views allows for the description of an identifiable object in the application from the three views. This is to say, that it is then possible to speak about one identified interaction object from different perspectives, and while the perspectives may not share a single common attribute in regard to their perception (and subsequently, their description) of the interaction object, they can be certain that they are referring to the same entity.

4.3.1 RM-IOS - Foundation

The RM-IOS foundation includes those model elements which are of fundamental and defining importance to an interaction oriented system. As these model elements are relevant to more than one, and often all perspectives and thus need to be accessible by all perspectives they are grouped in this section of RM-IOS.

The foundation builds on top of the RM-ODP foundation in that it utilizes the powerful, encompassing structure laid out in RM-ODP foundations. This is realized by linking between RM-IOS and RM-ODP. The two linked elements are the *object* entity in the RM-ODP foundation, and the the *interaction object* (see 5.2.16) in the RM-IOS, which inherits - from an object oriented perspective - from the *object* entity.

This approach at once provides an *interaction object* with all attributes and relations to the elements in the RM-ODP foundation that the *object* entity of RM-ODP possesses. Building the Reference Model for Interaction Oriented Systems thusly on top of the RM-ODP foundation, immediately provides the entire model with an industry-standard grade basis. Of course not all, and as a matter of fact only a minority of the elements in the RM-ODP foundation are relevant or useful to the modeling of an interaction oriented system in the style that the model structure of RM-IOS proposes. But the decision to leave the RM-ODP foundation intact - as opposed to making a selection of absolutely relevant model elements - was based mainly on three reasons:

1. With many elements there is no clear cut decision possible on whether an element is or might be useful for interaction oriented system modeling or not.

2. When weighing the two possible scenarios of needing an element that has been left out, or including an element that might never be of any use at all, the latter seems much less problematic.

3. Appreciating RM-ODP as a fundamentally solid model and considering the possibility of the arising need to extend RM-IOS, the basis, i.e. the RM-ODP foundation in this case, should be broad enough to support whatever extensions might become necessary. The RM-ODP foundation in its entirety provides such a broad and sound basis.

One of the key defining elements of the RM-IOS is the concept of the scene (see 5.2.2) as a snapshot of the state of the current user interface. Scenes are changed by interaction objects which act as scene triggers, i.e. an interaction object will trigger the moving from the current scene into another one. This scene element and all its related elements is part of the foundation, as in order to communicate an interaction oriented system among one another all perspectives need access to this element.

The RM-IOS foundation is not at all to be understood as an abstract background to the other three parts, the perspectives, of the RM-IOS. Instead, the foundation constitutes a common vocabulary to all three perspectives.

4.3.2 RM-IOS - Functionality

The RM-IOS functionality perspective provides model elements that serve as a link into the user interface development for the backend developing, i.e. the programming of the internal processes and services, of the application. Guided by the principle thought, that the functionality offered by any application can be characterized by answering the two questions "what input is needed by the system from the user?" and "what output is being provided by the system to the user?", the functionality perspective holds model elements needed to describe the answers to those questions.

The anchoring, model transcending, and perspective linking element here, too, is the *interaction object*, which gets extended by a definition relevant to the functionality perspective. The focus of this perspective then is, as just mentioned, the answering of the two questions stated above which is realized by providing model elements for input from the user and output to the user, respectively.

The reason for the RM-IOS functionality perspective to appear particularly minimalistic, is the fact that when working with the functionality perspective many of the elements of the foundation are also being used; another reason is the fact, that the backend developing actually should have little impact on the user interface. As the user does not care whether his data is being transmitted via WLAN, UMTS, Bluetooth, Infrared, or Ethernet. He also does not care what kind of database is being accessed for the retrieval of the information he requested. But these are typical development decisions that need to be made by the backend developers of an interaction oriented system. And for such decisions, i.e. for the technical development approach of applications in general, ample approaches, modeling tools (see UML, for that matter), and methodologies exist, as the entire information technology sector stems from the technical, functionality oriented approach.

While the duplication of the *Input Type* and *Output Type* in the foundation and functionality perspective may seem redundant at first glance, a closer inspection shows a crucial difference between the two perspectives: in the foundation, an input (or output) *may* have an input (or output) type, while in the functionality perspective this relationship is mandatory, i.e. every input (or output) *must* have an input (or output) type.

This difference may seem a bit trivial at first, however, it changes the way a system can be modeled significantly. In the foundation, the general input (and output) may be discussed, at this point, without regard for input (or output) types. But when the modeling is done from the functionality perspective, these aspects must then be decided and modeled respectively.

4.3.3 RM-IOS - Interaction

The RM-IOS interaction perspective is concerned with the questions "how a user provides input to the system" and "how a system presents output to the user". These questions complement the questions asked in the functionality perspective of "what" input and output is needed and offered respectively. While the functionality perspective is mostly a perspective used as an interface for the backend programming, the interaction perspective offers some fundamental modeling elements in the realm of user interface interaction. One of which is the aspect of the modality, which by being disconnected from the technical matter of data exchange allows for free and creative contemplation on which modality might be the best for the situation at hand.

The model elements "mode of operation" and "mode of presentation" then define the actual kind of interaction, based on whichever modality has been decided on.

A core concept introduced in the RM-IOS interaction perspective is the concept of *perceptibility* and *perceivability*. While no distinction is being made between those two terms in the english language, RM-IOS defines them distinctly different from one another.

In RM-IOS the term "perceptibility" refers to the possibility of a certain user being able to percept a signal under ideal conditions, i.e. when the signal is strong enough to be registered by a user's sense, the signal is perceptible. The term "perceivability" then examines a signal that is perceptible under several environmental conditions, i.e. with the typical noise of the environment overlaying and thus distracting from the signal. Obviously a signal must be perceptible to possibly be perceivable, and, following, a signal can not be perceivable without being perceptible.

The distinction between these two model elements allows for the modeling of different environmental conditions and is a concept that is currently not present in any of the prevalent models available to the domain of user interface design and development.

Note that model elements grouped in the interaction perspective are independent of[5] the modeling decisions in the functionality perspective. This created policy of separation of concern allows for independent modeling, and effectively, modifying, of the elements regarding the different domains of responsibility, and areas of expertise.

4.3.4 RM-IOS - Style

The main question the RM-IOS style perspective is concerned with is "what is the aesthetic styling of the interaction objects". To answer this question several model elements are being provided, which are the most dominant and obvious aspects in regard to a certain modality. The provision of this third perspective effectively removes the responsibility of styling from the functionality and, especially, the interaction perspective. Again, this realizes another policy of separation of concern by which the responsibilities regarding the decisions in the user interface development process are distributed according to currently predominant areas of expertise, i.e. graphic and audio designers can contribute their knowledge into the user interface development process by using the elements offered by the RM-IOS style perspective.

The existence of the RM-IOS style perspective constitutes a clear separation of aspects regarding the actual *interaction* and aspects regarding the *styling* thereof, continuing the often successfully realized philosophy that aspects of style should be separated from other aspects of a system[6].

It must be acknowledged that the author is aware of the fact, that the style perspective is particularly incomplete and should be considered as an extensible foundation. As art of design is not the author's field of expertise, it seemed prudent to only lay the fundamental basics for this perspective and refrain from making the presumptuous attempt of modeling something the author has only rudimental knowledge of. This fact, however, does not compromise the reasoning behind the conceptual creation

---

[5]The term *independent* here must not be confused with the term *uninfluenced*, as obviously the kind of data being needed and provided by the system is of fundamental importance to the decisions made regarding the interaction with the system.

[6]This concept is one of the earlier concepts in the software engineering field, and can, for example, be found in the MVC paradigm (see 3.3.1) or the separation of website structure and logic in HTML and its appearance in CSS.

of the style perspective as the other two perspectives are sound in their structure and the separation of style related aspects is a widely accepted concept in any software development technique.

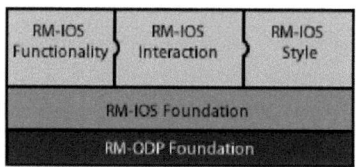

Figure 4.5: RM-IOS Architecture

4.3.5 Coverage of the RM-IOS

The just described perspectives of the Reference Model for Interaction Oriented Systems inherently synthesize a policy of separation of concern regarding the domains of skill and responsibilities in the domain of user interface development. One risk of realizing such a policy of separation of concern obviously is the incomplete coverage of the whole which is being separated. To assess the coverage of the three perspectives introduced here the complete area of responsibility generated by the sum of perspectives can be checked against the responsibilities during the user interface development process as stated by, for example, Galitz [Gal07].

As the development process of the Reference Model for Interaction Oriented Systems is based mainly on the "golden rules" by Shneiderman, and the entire development process can be retraced back to those rules there is no need for a direct mapping there. However, Galitz' suggested approach to user interface development is also interesting to include here as it provides a very different perspective than that presented by Shneiderman's "golden rules", with a somewhat chronological aspect to it. The approach advocated by Galitz is given in the following list:

- Know your User or Client
- Understand the Business Function
- Understand the Principle of Good Interface and Screen Design
- Develop System Menus and Navigation Schemes
- Select the Proper Kinds of Windows

- Select the Proper Interaction Devices
- Choose the Proper Screen-Based Controls
- Write Clear Text and Messages
- Provide Effective Feedback and Guidance and Assistance
- Provide Effective Internationalization and Accessibility
- Create Meaningful Graphics, Icons, and Images
- Choose the Proper Colors
- Organize and Layout Windows and Pages
- Test, Test, and Retest

When inspecting this list and holding it up against the three perspectives and their responsibilities as proposed here by the Reference Model for Interaction Oriented Systems it shows that the list by Galitz is being completely covered. In the table the column labeled "F" stands for the functionality perspective, the column labeled "I" stands for the interaction perspective, and "S" stands for the style perspective. A bullet is placed in those rows where a step falls into the area of responsibility of that perspective.

The reasoning behind the distribution of the responsibilities of the steps proposed by Galitz to the three perspectives of the Reference Model for Interaction Oriented Systems is self-explanatory from the descriptions of the three perspectives given prior to this section.

Additionally to the bottom-up evaluation of the completeness of the Reference Model for Interaction Oriented Systems by the anchoring of its development in Shneiderman's "golden rules", this table reaffirms from a top-down perspective that a complete view on the user interface development is being provided when combining all three perspectives.

4.4 RM-IOS - Six Questions for a Model

The description of the Reference Model for Interaction Oriented Systems concludes with the answering of six questions. The answers to these questions provide an overview of the meta-structure

STEPS PROPOSED BY GALITZ	F	I	S
Know Your User and Client	•	•	•
Understand the Business Function	•	•	•
Understand the Principles of Good Interface and Screen Design		•	•
Develop System Menus and Navigation Schemes		•	•
Select the Proper Kinds of Windows		•	•
Select the Proper Interaction Device		•	
Choose the Proper Screen-Based Controls		•	
Write Clear Text and Messages			•
Provide Effective Feedback and Guidance and Assistance		•	•
Provide Effective Internationalization and Accessibility	•	•	
Create Meaningful Graphics, Icons, and Images			•
Choose the Proper Colors			•
Organize and Layout Windows and Pages		•	•
Test, Test, and Retest	•	•	•

Table 4.1: RM-IOS' Perspectives in Galitz' Approach to UI Development

of a model and thereby unmistakably position the model and define the legitimacy of the research efforts invested into it. Also the problem domain and the solution domain are addressed in the last two questions.

4.4.1 Questions for a model

According to Mahr's concept of a model in [Mah08], the two core questions any model must be able to answer are the questions "what is the model a model of" and "what is the model a model for"[7]. In each of the answers to these questions lies one half of the dual nature of any model. While giving the answers to these two questions respectively might appear mundane, that would only be the case when formulating very generic, and thus imprecise answers[8]. These would then not be helpful at all,

---

[7]Mahr dissects these two questions even further by exposing the existence of a model's *cargo*, but for the purpose of this thesis, this depth is not necessary and can be reduced to the two questions just stated.

[8]For example by answering the two questions with: "a model of interaction oriented systems" and "a model for interaction oriented systems".

as the answers to these questions position the model in the perception of the user and thus preload his view on the model with certain expectations regarding the purpose, subsequently following, the utility of the model.

A third question a model can be queried with is the question "who is the model for". As the answer to that question helps to illuminate why certain modeling decisions have been thus made, and also legitimates the existence of the model in respect to its intended purpose; an especially plausible point for a model that aims to be of real, applied use, such as this Reference Model for Interaction Oriented Systems. The fourth question then, the counterpart to the third, is the question "whom is the model from" and should help furthering an understanding of the structural peculiarities of a model in respect to what knowledge and mental tools were available to the creator of the model.

The answers to these questions then should serve as, both, a mental outline that is drawn and background that is painted in which the actual model can then be viewed, inspected, and understood as closely to its intended purpose as possible. Additionally it seems equally important to state explicitly what this Reference Model for Interaction Oriented Systems is not a model of or for and these will be weaved into the answers of the just listed questions.

The following paragraphs now try to offer all these answers and descriptions.

What is RM-IOS a model of?

RM-IOS is a descriptive, perspective based model of the nature of the entities, their relations to one another, and the resulting structures in an interaction oriented system. It provides a generic, abstract structure, i.e. meta-structure, which describes the external functions and services available to the user of the interaction oriented system, the means available to the user to interact with the system, thus accessing the provided functions and services, and the way these are presented to him from an aesthetic point of view.

It is not a model of a particularly good or lauded interaction oriented system and as such does not include any qualitative assessments. Rather it is a lexical reference that describes certain *invariable aspects of any* interaction oriented system. It is also especially not a model of a development process or any methodology for that matter. It is not a model of a certain technical realization of an interaction oriented system, that is to say, that in effect the Reference Model for Interaction Oriented Systems itself is independent of any implementation or technical realization.

What is RM-IOS a model for?

RM-IOS is a descriptive, perspective based model for describing (i.e. modeling) interaction oriented systems, which can then be utilized for the specification, verification, analysis, comparison, and evaluation of interaction oriented systems.

It is not a model for modeling the internal functions and services of an interactive oriented system, but merely includes elements to model the external functions and services of an interactive oriented system. While the user is being part of the model, the Reference Model for Interaction Oriented Systems does not serve the purpose of user modeling as done by other models, for example the Personas model approach by Alan Cooper [CRC07]. Furthermore, the Reference Model for Interaction Oriented Systems does not provide the means for environment modeling. Certain model elements appreciate the influence the environment can have on the usability of a system, i.e. the effect of noise on the perceivability of audio signals emitted by the system, however, these model elements are neither meant nor suitable for extensive environment modeling.

Who is RM-IOS for?

It is the author's sincere hope that the model will be for the benefit of the end-user of interaction oriented systems, in that the model's contribution is beneficial to the user interface development process. However, the end-user will in most cases never have anything to do with this model. But this ambition and view is a perspective the author thinks is important to maintain in order to not fall into an overly technology oriented perspective.

That being said, the model effectively is for those people directly involved in the user interface development process, i.e. engineers, software developers, designers, and interaction specialists[9]. These experts from different domains should hopefully find the Reference Model for Interaction Oriented Systems helpful when describing, specifying, verifying, analyzing, evaluating, comparing, and - fundamentally important - communicating about and their view on interaction oriented systems with one another.

---

[9]One could argue that an "interaction specialist" must be all of those combined, and surely the newly found discipline of interaction specialists will be adequately versed in all scientific fields relevant to user interface development; enough to have a holistic view on the design and development of user interfaces. However, there will probably always be the software developer likely with a background in computer science or programming, and the designer likely with a background in graphical or animated arts who will also be part of the user interface development process.

Whom is RM-IOS from?

The creator of the model has a background in computer science, with a focus on formal models and modeling methodologies. Thus the dominant perspective throughout the creation of the model was one mainly from an engineering point of view. From this fact several observations about the creation of this model can be made, i.e. about the procedural method of creating this model and the nature and quality of the model itself. The author himself draws his own conclusions and offers them to the reader in section 5.7.

What is RM-IOS' problem domain?

In engineering disciplines the term "problem domain" is used to identify the relevant aspects and areas of expertise needed to examine the topics central to solving the challenge posed by the circumstance of interest.

Defining the problem domain of a situation of interest immediately determines the direction and characteristics of the solution approach[10]. Also, the definition of the problem domain affixes the criteria the solution will have to be held up against in order to decide, whether the proposed solution actually addresses the challenges posed by the elements of the problem domain or is just *a* solution possibly to a completely different problem (see [Jac01] for a discussion of the importance of a well understood and defined problem domain in the realm of software development).

The following aspects constitute the problem domain of the Reference Model for Interaction Oriented Systems introduced in this thesis:

- the conceptual and analytical part of user interface development

- the abilities and limitations of the user's perception

- the system the user interacts with, in particular the functionality the system offers to the user, the way in which the user interacts with the system, and the aesthetic aspects of the presentation of the system to the user

---

[10]This is not to be confused with the actual solution as to one challenge and its identified problem domain generally several solutions are possible. However, the problem domain does strongly influence the solution as what has not been included in the definition of the problem domain will obviously not be considered during the finding of a suitable solution.

- the communication between the different domains of skill and expertise needed during the user interface development process, and recognition of the different areas of responsibility based on those skill sets

What is RM-IOS' solution domain?

Contrary to the problem domain, the solution domain is not so much a matter of a preset definition, but rather comprises the entirety of all possible solutions to the challenges posed by the problem domain. The particular solution proposed to answer to the problem domain, in this case the Reference Model for Interaction Oriented Systems and its construction is one possible solution of all conceivable solutions.

The solution offered in this thesis comprises a perspective based reference model that has been created by following a rational, analytical approach to the problem domain and in its underlying structure has followed the style of and includes aspects from the reference model of open distributed processing (RM-ODP).

In an attempt to realize the fundamental concept of a useful Reference Model for Interaction Oriented Systems, namely that "[...]a good reference model should provide a structure which is common to all user interface support systems" (a suggestion made by Lynch and Meads [LM86]) the herein proposed model focuses on the timeless, technology-independent meta-aspects of a user interface and the user's interaction with it.

Chapter 5

Reference Model for Interaction Oriented Systems

5.1 RM-IOS

This chapter presents the reference model for interaction oriented system which has been created for this thesis.

It contains the actual model with the following section 5.6 providing a structural overview of the entire model by presenting four UML class diagrams, each depicting one of the parts of the model. These diagrams are intended to provide a quick graphical overview of the entire structure of the model and should help to approach the model.

5.2 Foundation

5.2.1 Interaction Oriented System

Definition

An interaction oriented system can be described by a non-empty set of scenes belonging to one system.

Explanation

Defining an interaction oriented system by including it as an element of the Reference Model for Interaction Oriented Systems provides the anchoring element in the problem domain the Reference Model for Interaction Oriented Systems offers one solution for. The concept behind an interaction oriented system then is the entirety of a system the user interacts with in regard to the three perspectives of functionality, interaction, style. It comprises software and hardware elements alike, and thus is not reduced to a mere description of the interaction elements presented on a display. All elements available to the user, whether virtual as software elements, or actual as hardware elements, are part of the description of an interaction oriented system.

The inclusion and equalization of hardware elements and software elements allows for an encompassing description of interaction elements available to the user and thus allows for a holistic description of the possible interaction with a system.

Example

The interaction elements of a smartphone, i.e. the virtual elements on the screen and the actual elements on the device itself are an example of an interaction oriented system. Such an interaction oriented system is being examined in the case study in chapter 6. Another example for an interaction oriented system is the cockpit of a car where in contemporary cars the majority of interaction elements still are hardware interaction elements. The classic desktop computer with its immense versatility achieved by being able to run a plethora of different applications is, of course, also an example for an interaction oriented system.

5.2.2 Scene

Definition

A scene is a set of interaction objects available to the user at a certain location in time and a certain state of the interaction oriented system. The interaction objects of a scene have a distinct spatial relation to one another. A scene is activated by a scene triggering interaction object. A scene is not empty. The set of all scenes of an interaction oriented system comprises all possible interactions with the system.

Explanation

An interaction oriented system must be structured in such a way that it enables the use of the Reference Model for Interaction Oriented Systems during the analysis and synthesis of it. The scene concept provides this structure by allowing the modeler to create suitable "snapshots" of the interaction oriented system. The "non-emptiness" of a scene must not be confused with a situation, where a scene may not present any visible interaction objects to the user, thus *appearing* empty.

Example

An obvious scene is the single window of a "wizard"-dialogue. The user is presented with a set of interaction objects and upon clicking the "next" button is taken to a new scene. Also, the screen of a smartphone at a certain moment during the using of an app is a good example of a scene. However, a scene is not limited to the virtual elements on the screen but can also include the available hardware interaction elements of a device. An example of a scene can be found in the case study of this thesis starting on page 114 ff.

5.2.3 User

Definition

A person who uses the services offered by an interaction oriented system by providing input and being the designated receiver of the output. The user does not have to be a single real person but can be understood as a certain class of users.

Explanation

Every interaction oriented system must communicate with a user through the transfer of input and output. And during the modeling of a system the user will typically have to be defined, as a well defined user is of fundamental importance to designing a satisfying user-experience. The modeling of the user itself, however, is not part of this reference model, as other, well established models and approaches already exist. But during the modeling of a system with this reference model the user will be a model-element that needs to be referred to and included in modeling the interaction processes with the system.

User modeling is a discipline of its own and several methods exist (for example the "Personas" approach [CRC07]) for this task. It is not part of this model to cover techniques of user modeling but in the context of this model, the user is *part of the model* but *not part of the system*. A system is built with a certain user in mind and different users come with different abilities and requirements which can, among other aspects, affect the perceptibility and perceivability of system elements.

Example

A class of users could be defined as people between 50-60 years of age, with none to limited technical background knowledge and experience. Another example would be a group of users between 14-16 years of age, with a strong technical background.

5.2.4 Input

Definition

Information exchanged between the system and the user where the information is provided to the system by the user through interaction objects.

Explanation

Whenever a user interacts with a system some sort of input is required to yield the output generated by the system. As such, input is the parameter to the offered functionality of a system.

Example

The PIN users type at an ATM, their name entered in a web-form, the numbers punched in on a dial-pad, the selection of a ticket from a public-transportation ticket-vending machine, the biometric data scanned from their fingertip placed a biometric scanner, the gesture made into a camera, the spoken word into a microphone, all are examples of input.

5.2.5 Output

Definition

Information exchanged between the system and the user where the information is provided to the user by the system through interaction objects.

Explanation

For a system to be of any use at all, some sort of output must be provided. In that output lies the essence of the system's offered functionality.

Example

Presenting the result of a calculation, offering several buttons to make some sort of choice, vibrating and ringing on an incoming call, displaying a little icon that notifies the user that the system is currently busy all are examples of output.

5.2.6 Maximum Value

Definition

If an input or output is limited to a highest possible value, then this is the maximum value.

Explanation

While some input is being entirely unrestricted, often there is a limit constraining the possible input. If the limit is or can be understood as a top limit, it is the maximum limit. This does not only relate to numerical input but can be specified in a more abstract way.

Example

The most obvious example is a numerical restriction, i.e. limiting an input to a highest possible number. But a date is also limited to a selection of twelve months. And the ability to upscale an image could be restricted to a certain size, thus imposing a maximum limit on the pixel size of the scaling.

5.2.7 Minimum Value

Definition

If an input or output is limited to a lowest possible value, then this is the minimum value.

Explanation

While some output is being entirely unrestricted, often there is a limit constraining the possible output. If the limit is or can be understood as a bottom limit, it is the minimum limit. This does not only relate to numerical input but can be specified in a more abstract way.

Example

The most obvious example is a numerical restriction, i.e. limiting an input to a lowest possible number. But requiring the user to provide at least one value of a selection, or restricting the output of an image to be at least of a certain size are also examples for a more abstract minimum value.

5.2.8 Input Range

Definition

Input can be limited to a minimum and/or maximum value. The range of values in between is the input range.

Explanation

Input that is restricted by, both, a minimum and maximum value is confined to the input range defined by those two limits. The most obvious case would be a restriction to a numerical range, but also more abstract situations are possible, where a range is defined by the enumeration of input objects.

Example

Restricting input to, for example, a number between 1 to 10 is a very obvious input range. But also the restriction of input to the letters of a certain alphabet is a preset input range definition. The same holds true for being able to resize an image to a certain maximal and certain minimal size.

5.2.9 Output Range

Definition

Output can be limited to a minimum and/or maximum value. The range of values in between is the output range.

Explanation

Output that is restricted by, both, a minimum and maximum value is confined to the output range defined by those two limits. The most obvious case would be a restriction to a numerical range, but also more abstract situations are possible, where a range is defined by the enumeration of output objects.

Example

Defining output to, for example, a number between 1 to 10 is a very obvious output range. But also the restriction of output to the letters of a certain alphabet is a preset output range definition. An image, that is never going to be displayed smaller or larger than a certain size is another example for a restricting output range.

5.2.10 Selection

Definition

A selection is a defined set of data typically used for specifying all possible input or all possible output.

Explanation

When the possible input or output is limited to a certain selection of data it is useful to be aware of this selection as it can strongly influence the kind of required interaction. This model element focuses the awareness during the modeling process towards this potential situation and allows for specification of selections during the conception of the system.

Example

Unicode symbols, alphanumerical symbols, the three values "red, green, blue" or "on, off, stand-by" are example for predefined selections of input or output.

5.2.11 Input Modality

Definition

The mapping of input to a certain kind of sensor or device of the computer.

Explanation

Input must be provided by means of at least one input modality. Depending on the situation and use-context some input modality might be better suited than another.

Example

Entering text by pressing the keys on a keyboard, or speaking the text into a microphone are two examples for haptic and audio input modality.

5.2.12 Output Modality

Definition

The mapping of output to one of the human senses.

Explanation

The system must utilize at least one output modality in order to present output to the user. Depending on the situation and use-context some output modality might be better suited than another.

Example

Todays most common output modalities are the visual modality, i.e. presenting output on a display, and audio modality, i.e. playing sounds. Haptic modality output can often be found in controllers for video-games via vibrating, and vibrating is also commonly found in cell phone devices to indicate for example an incoming message or incoming call. Other output modalities such as gustation, olfaction, and thermoception modalities are not part of contemporary systems.

5.2.13 Input Type

Definition

The type of input in terms of its nature.

Explanation

Once an abstract conception of a system is being concretized, an input type for the input must be defined. Input types could be "string", "number", but also more complex and composite types such as "date", "address", or any other application specific data type. A composite input type is an input type comprising other input types. A complex input type is an input type which composition will not be explained further at the scope of modeling.

Example

A name is a simple input of type string. An address is a composite input of type address which in turn comprises strings and numbers. A biometrical fingerprint is a complex input which internal structure is not being dissected at the current scope of modeling.

5.2.14 Output Type

Definition

The type of output in terms of its nature. Output types could be "string", "number", but also more complex and composite types such as "date", "address", or any other application specific data type.

Explanation

Once an abstract conception of a system is being concretized, an output type for the output must be concretized. Output types could be "string", "number", but also more complex and composite types such as "date", "address", or any other application specific data type. A composite output type is an input type comprising other input types. A complex output type is an output type which composition will not be explained further at the scope of modeling.

Example

A name is a simple output of type string. An address is a composite output type comprising strings and numbers. A picture is a complex output type whose structure is not further modeled at the current scope.

5.2.15 Stream

Definition

A stream is an input type or output type that is continuous over a period of time. A stream typically has an inherent chronicity that must be adhered to in order to not alter the information significantly.

Explanation

Data such as music or a movie can obviously not be presented "at once" but instead needs to be input or output continuously over a period of time.

Example

A two-way video conference is an example of a visual and audio input and output where the data captured by the camera and the microphone need to be received and presented continuously.

5.2.16 Interaction Object

Definition

An interaction object is an object that receives input or presents output. An interaction object can contain one or more interaction objects.

Explanation

An element in the user interface that receives input or presents output is an interaction object. Depending on the viewpoint an interaction object possesses different attributes. Functionality attributes from the functionality viewpoint, interaction attributes from the interaction viewpoint, and style attributes from the style viewpoint. This is the basis for letting one identifiable element being modeled from the three distinct perspectives with different interests depending on the viewpoint.

Example

A virtual button on the user interface is a (graphical) interaction object, the ringtone of a cellphone is a (acoustical) interaction object, a real button on a keyboard is a (haptical) interaction object, and a touchscreen is a (graphical and haptical) interaction object.

5.2.17 Trigger

Definition

A trigger is an input type or output type which provides only the atomic information that it has occurred.

Explanation

Some input does not transfer entered information from the user to the system but merely allows the system to understand that some event has taken place.

Example

The user clicking a "send" button on a composed mail, pushing the hang-up button on a telephone, or activating a motion-sensor by moving are examples of trigger-inputs.

5.2.18 Scene Trigger

Definition

A scene trigger is a trigger that activates a new scene.

Explanation

Applications present themselves to the user as a collection of scenes. A scene change happens when upon the interaction with an object a new scene is being presented to the user. The interaction object that triggers that scene change is a scene trigger.

Example

A scene presents itself to the user as a virtual form, comprising textfields for input, a submit-button, and a cancel-button. Pressing the submit- or cancel-button causes the scene to change, as in the former case a scene will be presented to the user confirming the submission, and in the latter case a scene will be presented to the user confirming the cancellation of the form. The submit- and the cancel- button in this case both are scene triggers.

5.3 Functionality Viewpoint

The functionality viewpoint describes the system's aspects relevant to the provided functionality. This is accomplished by describing the system as a black-box that is defined solely by the system's input and output exchange, i.e. the answers to the two questions:

- What input does the system require?
- What output does the system provide?

5.3.1 Interaction Object

Definition

An interaction object possesses functionality attributes.

Explanation

An interaction object in the user interface is a way to exchange input and output between the user and the system. The functionality viewpoint inspects such an interaction object on the basis of which input it is to receive or which output it is to present.

Example

A text-field is an interaction object for a user to enter, for example, his name. A button is an interaction object for a user, for example, to trigger sending a message. A non-editable text-field is an interaction object for the system to, for example, display the result of a calculation.

5.3.2 Input

Definition

Information exchanged between the system and the user where the information is provided to the system by the user. Input is a functionality attribute. Input is of a certain input type. Input may be limited by a minimum and/or maximum value or by a selection.

Explanation

Whenever a user interacts with a system some sort of input is required to yield the output generated by the system. As such, input is the parameters to the offered functionality of a system.

Example

Users typing their PIN at an ATM machine, entering their name in a web-form, punching numbers on a dial-pad, selecting a ticket from a public-transportation ticket-vending machine, placing their finger on a biometric scanner all are examples of input.

5.3.3 Output

Definition

Information exchanged between the system and the user where the information is provided to the user by the system. Output is of a certain output type. Output may be limited by a minimum and/or maximum value.

Explanation

From the functionality viewpoint output is a matter of output type and possibly an output range associated with it. Whenever a user interacts with a system some sort of output is being generated by the system. This output effectively provides the functionality of the system.

Example

A calculator provides the result of the request calculation as output. A navigation system provides an overview of an area and driving directions. A music-player outputs the name of the song and album, and the sound.

5.3.4 Input Type

Definition

The type of input in terms of its nature.

Explanation

Input types could be "string", "number", but also more complex and composite types such as "date", "address", or any other application specific data type. A composite input type is an input type comprising other input types. A complex input type is an input type which composition will not be explained further at the scope of modeling.

Example

A name is a simple input of type string. An address is a composite input of type address which in turn comprises strings and numbers. A biometrical fingerprint is a complex input which internal structure is not being dissected at the current scope of modeling.

5.3.5 Output Type

Definition

The type of output in terms of its nature. Output types could be "string", "number", but also more complex and composite types such as "date", "address", or any other application specific data type.

Explanation

Output types could be "string", "number", but also more complex and composite types such as "date", "address", or any other application specific data type. A composite output type is an input type comprising other input types. A complex output type is an output type which composition will not be explained further at the scope of modeling.

Example

A name is a simple output of type string. An address is a composite output type comprising strings and numbers. A picture is a complex output type whose structure is not further modeled at the current scope.

5.4 Interaction Viewpoint

Describing the aspects of a system relevant to the interactability and usability of the system.

5.4.1 Interaction Object

Definition

An interaction object possesses interaction attributes.

Explanation

An interaction object in the user interface is a way to exchange input and output between the user and the system. The interaction viewpoint inspects such an interaction object on the basis of how input is to be entered and how output is to be presented.

Example

A turn-knob is an interaction object that will be turned by the user to receive the user's input. A slider is an interaction object that will be moved from one end of its scale to the other to receive the user's input. Both interaction objects could be used for the same task, i.e. adjusting volume, but one might be better suited from the interaction viewpoint than the other.

5.4.2 Input

Definition

Input is an interaction attribute. Input is information exchanged between the system and the user where the information is provided to the system by the user. Input has at least one input modality.

Explanation

Whenever a user interacts with a system some sort of input is required to yield the output generated by the system. As such, input is the parameters to the offered functionality of a system. From the interaction viewpoint the interest in input lies in how it is being entered, i.e. the input modality.

Example

The user pushing keys on a keyboard, tapping a certain location on the screen, or speaking into a microphone are all examples of input.

5.4.3 Output

Definition

Output is an interaction attribute. Output is information exchange between the system and the user where the information is provided to the user by the system. Output has at least one input modality.

Explanation

The one reason why a system is being used and a user interacts with it, i.e. provides input, is the output a system is able to generate. With the system seen as a "blackbox" the output is what lets a user make assumptions about the working of the system. Thus output can either have feedback character, i.e. to inform the user about an accepted interaction attempt, or can deliver the result of input manipulation to the user.

Example

A screen showing a picture, or a textbox displaying a name, the speaker of a navigation system emitting the driving-directions, or the vibrating of a cell phone on an incoming message are examples of output.

5.4.4 Feedback

Definition

Output that immediately follows the provision of input to confirm the act of providing input.

Explanation

The user has per se no way of telling whether her interaction with the system has been registered by the system. Feedback is needed to inform the user that her action has been registered.

Example

A common kind of feedback is the visual change of state of a "pushed down" button. It informs the user that her action of pushing the button has been registered. The click sound emitted when pushing keys or activating interface elements is an example for audio feedback. Sometimes the functionality of an action already provides feedback in and by itself, like the letters that appear on the screen when a letter-key has been pushed.

5.4.5 Perceptibility

Definition

Perceptibility is an attribute of the relation between "input and the system" and "output and the user". Information exchanged is perceptible when the stimulus it triggers is within the boundaries of the user class senses' registration capability or the system device's registration capability respectively. The question of perceptibility is highly dependent on the innate abilities of the user and the technical sophistication level of the system.

Explanation

Free of impeding and overlapping noise a signal can be detectable by the human senses or not be detectable by the human senses. Assuming that a signal is being emitted in a distraction free environment, the question, whether that signal would be registered by the human senses of a user answers the perceptibility of that signal.

Example

The sound generated by blowing into a dog whistle is not perceptible by the human ear, the sound generated by activating a car's horn is perceptible by the human ear. A microscopically small dot is not perceptible by the human eye, the dot at the end of this sentence is perceptible by the human eye.

5.4.6 Perceivability

Definition

Perceivability is an attribute of the relation between an "input and the system" and "output and the user". Information exchanged is perceivable when the interferences of the environment do not eliminate its perceptibility.

Explanation

Given the premise of perceptibility of a signal the environmental noise (not necessarily acoustical noise) may make it imperceivable to the human sense, overlaying the signal or distracting from it. Thus, perceivability here is defined as the ability of an object to trigger a sufficient sensory stimulus. The question of perceivability is highly dependent on the innate abilities of the user.

Example

A word spoken at regular volume is a perceptible event, however, spoken next to a starting jet-plane it becomes imperceivable. A needle is a visually perceptible object, however, in the proverbial haystack its perceivability becomes extremely diminished.

5.4.7 Visibility

Definition

Visibility describes the visual perceptibility of an interaction object to a user.

Visibility is only concerned with the actual visibility state of an interaction object and not used to describe whether a layout situation prevents an interaction object from being seen or not because of an entity blocking the line-of-sight (see 5.4.8).

Explanation

Perceptibility is the general term for describing the ability of a user's senses to register a sensory stimulus. The term visibility now is concerned only with the *visual perceptibility* of an object, thus, per definition, it applies only to objects which trigger a visual stimulus.

Example

Any object that emits or reflects light is an object which can be evaluated regarding its visibility to the user.

5.4.8 Viewability

Definition

Viewability describes the visual perceivability of an interaction object, i.e. if the line-of-sight is not being obstructed by something else, or if the environmental visual distraction allows for the object to still be perceived.

Explanation

An object can be visible to the user but due to issues of viewing angle of the display, obstructed line of sight, overly distracting visual noise the object becomes non-viewable. The question of viewability is highly dependent on the innate abilities of the user.

Example

A black line drawn with a ballpoint pen on a white paper is from a distance of 30cm, both, visible and viewable. The same black line drawn on a black paper is most likely non-viewable, as the contrast to the background is not sufficient enough. The keypad for entering the pin number at an ATM machine is clearly visible, but the flaps attached to it to prevent others from watching the user entering her PIN number makes it non-viewable.

5.4.9 Audibility

Definition

Audibility describes the auditory perceptibility of a signal.

Explanation

The human ear is being attributed with being able to hear audio signals within a range of 12 Hz to 20,000 Hz [Ols67, p. 249], although that range shrinks over the lifetime of a human being. Thus, for a sound to be audible it must be within that range of pitch. The pitch of the sound generated by a dog whistle, for example, is above 20,000 Hz and thus not audible by the human ear.

Example

Sounds in the ultrasonic spectrum of sound are not audible by a human ear. The sound emitted by a car's horn is audible to the human ear.

5.4.10 Hearability

Definition

Hearability describes the auditory perceivability of a signal.

Explanation

Given the audibility of a signal for a user as a premise the hearability then describes whether that signal is also still audible in certain situations, i.e. the scenarios in which the system is being used. This attribute reminds of the fact, that a signal might be audible when emitted in a silent environment but that given a certain scenario the environmental noise might drown the signal, thus, rendering it useless.

Example

The beeping tone of an incoming message on a cellphone is an audible signal as it is loud enough to be heard and in a silent room it is hearable. However, that beeping tone is being rendered nonhearable when emitted in a driving car with a turned up stereo-system, as the noise present in that situation is much louder than the beeping tone of the cell phone.

5.4.11 Tangibility

Definition

Tangibility describes the haptic perceptibility of an interaction object.

Explanation

When it is possible to touch an object that object is tangible.

Example

A turning knob is a tangible object, as it can be touched and felt. A virtual button on a touchscreen, however, is not tangible. The touchscreen itself is a tangible object but the button is not. Critically, depending on the modeling situation it might be sensible to model a button on a touchscreen as a tangible object, but the distinction is something that should be recognized while modeling.

5.4.12 Feelability

Definition

Feelability describes the haptic perceivability of an interaction object.

Explanation

When an interaction object is to be operated by touching manipulation, it is critical that the interaction object can be easily felt and handled by the user. The attribute of feelability allows for the modeling of this aspect.

Example

A button that is flush with the surface it is on is possibly not feelable to a user who is to operate it without looking. Tiny keys on a very small keyboard might also not be individually feelable.

Feelability is an aspect to be especially kept in mind when an interaction object is expected to be operated without the user actually looking at it, too.

5.4.13 Mode of Operation

Definition

Mode of operation is an interaction attribute and describes the nature of input an interaction object is able to receive.

Explanation

While the modality of an input interaction describes which of the human senses is involved, the mode of operation then describes the nature of the input interaction itself. A mode of operation is always a distinct way of receiving input in a given modality.

Example

A virtual button on a touch sensitive surface and an actual push-in button on some panel are both interactions in the realm of haptic modality. Yet they are obviously different as in the former case a certain area on a touch sensitive screen must be touched, in the latter a certain area must be actually moved, i.e. pushed in. Another example for two different mode of operations in the realm of haptic modality would be a slider along a one dimensional axis and turn knob that can be rotated.
An example in the realm of audio modality would be a light switch that is activated by a speaking a certain word, or activated by clapping the hands.
An example in the realm of visual modality would be holding up a bar code to a scanner or holding up a picture to a scanner.

5.4.14 Mode of Presentation

Definition

Mode of presentation is an interaction attribute and describes the nature of output an interaction object presents to the user.

Explanation

While the modality of an output interaction describes which of the human sense is involved, the mode of presentation then describes the nature of the output interaction itself. A mode of presentation is always a distinct way of presenting output in a given modality.

The mode of presentation effectively models the actual occurence of the modality-bound output.

Example

In the realm of visual modality an icon of a printer is a different mode of presentation than a text in a framed box reading "print".

In the realm of audio modality a beep sound is a different mode of presentation than a voice speaking a word.

5.5 Style Viewpoint

Describes the styling and presentation of a system.

5.5.1 Interaction Object

Definition

An interaction object possesses style attributes.

Explanation

An interaction object is an element of the user interface that possesses certain style attributes. The style viewpoint does not describe the functionality that is associated with a certain interaction element, although that is not to say that the functionality is being ignored. It merely says that it is not part of the style viewpoint, as the style viewpoint is concerned with how interaction elements are styled and present themselves to the user from an aesthetic point of view.

Example

When inspecting a virtual button, the action that will be triggered by pushing it is part of the functionality viewpoint, the fact that it is a virtual button that can be touched to be activated is part of the interaction viewpoint. The fact that it is of a certain color, has a certain shape, is placed at a certain location, these attributes are part of the style viewpoint of an interaction object.

5.5.2 Style Attributes

Definition

Style attributes allow for the modeling of attributes of an interaction object in dependence of a modality when inspected from the style viewpoint.

Explanation

An interaction object has several different attributes, which are grouped into the three perspectives: functionality, interaction, and style. Style attributes are those concerned with the appearance and general aesthetics of an interaction object.

Example

Style attributes of the haptic modality are concerned with the haptic appearance of an interaction object, for example 'rough', 'smooth', 'soft'. Style attributes of the visual modality are concerned with the visual appearance of an interaction object, for example 'blue', 'round', 'to the left of ...'. Style attributes of the audio modality are concerned with the audio appearance of an interaction object, for example 'loud', 'silent', 'fading'.

5.5.3 Haptic Style Attributes

Definition

Haptic style attributes describe the haptic appearance of an interaction object.

Explanation

Anything tangible has a certain haptic appearance. This haptic appearance can be described by haptic style attributes.

Example

The firmness of an object or the haptic texture (see 5.5.4) of its surface are both examples of haptic style attributes.

5.5.4 Haptic Texture

Definition

Haptic texture is a haptic style attribute and describes the feel of an interaction object's surface.

Explanation

Every physical object has a surface. The haptic texture describes the feel of that surface.

Example

A surface might be rough, grooved, or smooth. It could have a rubbery or a glossy touch.

5.5.5 Visual Style Attributes

Definition

Visual style attributes are style attributes perceptible by the human's optical sense or a computer's optical sensor.

Explanation

Every visible entity has certain visual attributes by which it can be described, specified, or identified. Any such attribute is a visual style attribute.

Example

In the realm of visual modality shape, color, placement, distance all are style aspects of an interaction object.

5.5.6 Color

Definition

Color is a visual style attribute and describes an interaction object's color.

Explanation

A visible entity can present itself in a certain color. Color is an important aspect in the styling of user interfaces, as certain colors are culturally identified with certain implication, i.e. red typically means "stop", "danger", "attention", where green typically means "go", "safe", "working" etc.

Example

The red color of a button, the green color of an LED, the blue color of a background are examples of the color attribute.

5.5.7 Iconic

Definition

Iconic is a visual style attribute and describes the iconic expression of a visual interaction object. If an interaction element possesses this attribute, it is an icon.

Explanation

Icons are small, simplified graphics. Icons are a prevalent aspect of graphical user interfaces (GUIs) where they are used as graphical labels to identify commands, applications, and file types.
Icons are one of the fundamental aspects of today's still widely used WIMP ("window, icon, menu, pointing device") interfaces. In the context of software based user interfaces, icons are little pictures that are used instead of words to distinctively convey a very specific meaning or give visual clues. Erwin Panofsky's "Meaning in the Visual Arts" [Pan83] offers a detailed discussion on the nature of icons.

Example

The small graphic of a printer on a button indicates that pressing this button will start some printing routine. A magnifying glass is commonly used to indicate some sort of search or zoom functionality. These graphics are iconic and have been used as classic icons in the WIMP interaction domain.

5.5.8 Shape

Definition

Shape is a visual and haptic style attribute and describes an interaction object's shape.

Explanation

The shape of an object is defined by the space the object occupies, either in 2D or 3D space.

Example

Round, rectangular, square, elliptical, are all examples of shapes commonly found in graphical user interfaces.

5.5.9 Size

Definition

Size is a visual and haptic style attribute and describes the dimensional expansion of an interaction object in at least one dimension. The size of all interaction objects of a scene together with their positioning are the two most important aspects concerning the scene and all its interaction objects and the available projection screen, i.e. typically a display.

Explanation

In graphical user interfaces the size of an interaction object is typically measured in pixels. The width and height in pixels of a virtual button then describes the size of that button in relation to the resolution the virtual button is being displayed on. Often the size of non-rectangular graphical objects are given by giving the size of an "invisible rectangle" the graphical object could be minimally contained by.

Example

250px high, 400px wide would be the size of a rectangle on any resolution. A round object of the same measure would be an ellipse. A hardware switch could be 4mm long and 2mm wide.

5.5.10 Position

Definition

Position is a visual and haptic style attribute and describes the location in space of an interaction object.

Explanation

Entities that have a visual representation occupy a certain location in space. On a two dimensional plane the location in space is biuniquely given by their ordinates along the vertical and horizontal axis. In a three dimensional room the location in space is biuniquely given by their ordinates along the vertical, horizontal, and depth axis. In contemporary user interfaces the two dimensional layout of user interface elements is still the most predominantly occurring visual layout. The user interface itself provides a certain appearance, composed by the positions of its user interface elements, i.e. their positions and distances to one another. While changing this spatial structure of user interface elements is at least impractical, often impossible in physical user interfaces, it happens very commonly in virtual, i.e. software user interfaces. Here two different kinds of change in positioning can be observed: elements changing their position but retaining their distance to certain other interface elements[1] and elements changing their position and the distance to certain other interface elements. The absolute position of interface elements in the user interface play a major role in the cognition of the user interface by the user and some interesting parallels can be observed between user interface layout design and the typeface theory, which - among other aspects of the written word - deals with the layout, kerning, size, and position of letters towards one another. The position of all interaction objects of a scene together with their size (see 5.5.9) are the two most important aspects concerning the scene and all its interaction objects and the available projection screen, i.e. typically a display.

Example

An absolute positioning could be "5 pixels from the top edge of the window, 20 pixels from the left edge of the window", whereas an example of a relative positioning could be "10 pixels to the left and 15 pixels above interaction object <x>".

---

[1] An example of this would be the scrolling of a website, where the elements "slide" up the screen, but their position towards one another remains intact.

5.5.11 Distance

Definition

Distance is a visual and haptic style attribute and describes the size of space between two interaction objects. It is a derived attribute caused by the position of two interaction objects. Distance is measured in a units of length.

Explanation

Distance is an essential aspect of user interface design and constitutes one of the fundamental laws of perception in cognition-psychology, namely the "law of proximity", which states that objects that are spatially grouped are perceived as belonging together [Met09]. This aspect finds its quintessential characteristic in the attribute of distance from one interaction object to one or many others. But besides the law of proximity distance also is important in the esthetic layout of the interface. The Apple Human Interface Guideline [Inc06] for example strongly recommends a margin of 20 pixels, which of course describes the distance of the side edge of a window to the closest inner interaction object. The distance attribute thus allows the specification and checking of such aspects of the interface.

Example

10 pixels between virtual button "A", and textfield "B" are an example of distance between two interaction elements.

5.5.12 Interval

Definition

Interval is a style attribute and describes the distance in time between two acts of information exchange. Interval is measure in units of time.

Explanation

Repetition of signals or events is often used in interaction oriented systems to increase the chance of raising a user's attention.

Example

The blinking of the cursor in a text-processing program is an example of an interval occurring in output. The double-click on a mouse is an example of an interval occurring in input. This blinking is defined by the interval, i.e. the time passing, between the disappearing and reappearing of the cursor. Same holds true for audio signals, for example, alarms and notifications.

5.5.13 Font

Definition

Font is a visual style attribute. It is a specific character set of a particular typeface in a specific size and of specific weight and defines the appearance of text.

Explanation

Text is a fundamental part of visual user interfaces. Whether it is the actual output that is being provided as text, or it is text occurring in the labeling of interaction elements. This text by definition has a certain appearance which is described by the font attribute.

Example

One of the most well-known fonts is the Arial typeface. "Arial, 12p, regular" would be an example of a font, namely, the typeface, the size, and the weight.

5.5.14 Terminology

Definition

Terminology is a visual or audio style attribute. Terminology is the specialized vocabulary or nomenclature for the words or compound words in the interface of an interaction oriented system.

Explanation

Shneiderman recommends the usage of a homogenous terminology in order not to confuse the user with different terms for same functionality or identical terms for different functionality. The terminology plays a vital part in the labeling of interface i.e. menu items.

Example

To "delete", "discharge", "erase", "destroy" a row in a table are different terms for (probably) the same functionality.

5.5.15 Audio Style Attributes

Definition

Audio style attributes are style attributes perceptible by the human's auditive sense or a computer's audio sensor.

Explanation

An audio signal can be described by its attributes. These attributes then are labeled audio style attributes.

Example

In the realm of the audio modality the particular sound of a voice speaking instructions of the user, or the particular clicking sound generated by a car's turning lights are examples for style aspects of an interaction object.

5.5.16 Pitch

Definition

Pitch is an audio style attribute. It defines the perceived frequency of a sound.

Explanation

The pitch of a sound is commonly described as the tone being high or low. Pitch is caused by the variation in the frequency of vibration.

Example

A high pitched sound or a low pitched sound could be descriptions of an alarm signal.

5.5.17 Timbre

Definition

Timbre is an audio style attribute. It describes the quality of a certain tone or sound.

Explanation

Timbre is what lets people distinguish between a piano and a trumpet both playing the same note. It has been said to be everything of a note that's not pitch or loudness. It is often described by using adjectives from other senses' domains [MB79].

Example

A sound's timbre can be warm, wooden, metallic, splashy, chirpy, mellow.

5.5.18 Loudness

Definition

Loudness is an audio style attribute. It describes the perceived volume of a sound.

Explanation

Loudness is not to be confused with strictly physical aspects of a sound such as sound pressure level. Rather, it is the perceived volume of a sound and thus is an inherently subjective aspect [Ins73].

Example

A sound can be perceived as loud or silent and anywhere in between. This is the loudness of a sound as perceived by someone.

5.5.19 Olfactory Style Attributes

Definition

Olfactory style attributes are concerned with the signals perceived by the human's sense for smell.

Explanation

While still almost non-existent in today's user interfaces, the aspect of scent is included here mostly for the sake of completion.

Example

Scent is typically described by naming objects associated with a typical scent, i.e. a scent can be leathery, or burnt, or fruity.

5.5.20 Gustatory Style Attributes

Definition

Gustatory style attributes are concerned with the attributes of taste.

Explanation

Equally irrelevant in contemporary user-interfaces as olfactoric interaction elements, the sense of taste is included here, also, mostly for the sake of completion.

Example

Salty, sweet, bitter, sour are examples of gustatory style attributes.

5.5.21 Thermoceptory Style Attributes

Definition

Thermoceptory style attributes are concerned with the perceived temperature of a signal.

Explanation

Thermoceptory signals are not part of contemporary user interfaces but are included here as a stub for the sake of completion.

Example

Warm, cold, chilly, tepid, are examples of thermoceptoric style attributes.

5.5.22 Equilibrioceptic Style Attributes

Definition

Equilibrioceptic style attributes are concerned with the balance and alignment of an object.

Explanation

With the advent of Nintendo's Wii console the aspect of balance and alignment has become an established aspect of user interaction, albeit with the Wii console almost exclusively in the realm of entertainment. Contemporary smartphones such as the Apple iPhone also make use of equilibrioceptic aspects by providing programs with the possibility to react to users moving and tilting their phone.

Example

A user rotating her smartphone onto the side, thus triggering the display to rotate $90°$, or steering an object on the display by tilting the phone along the two axis are examples of equilibrioceptic input.

An example of equilibrioceptic output is a car-simulator where the user sits inside a cabin and acceleration and deceleration is being simulating by tilting the cabin up and downwards, thus pressing the user into the back of the seat or out of the seat. In the isolated cabin where the eyes can not provide the additional information needed to clearly identify the reason for the felt change in pressure, this technique adds a very important component to the simulation, thus making it even more realistic.

5.6 Structural UML Class Diagrams of RM-IOS

Contained in this section are four UML class diagrams, each depicting one part of the RM-IOS:

- Figure 5.1 depicts the RM-IOS foundation
- Figure 5.2 depicts the RM-IOS functionality perspective
- Figure 5.3 depicts the RM-IOS interaction perspective
- Figure 5.4 depicts the RM-IOS style perspective

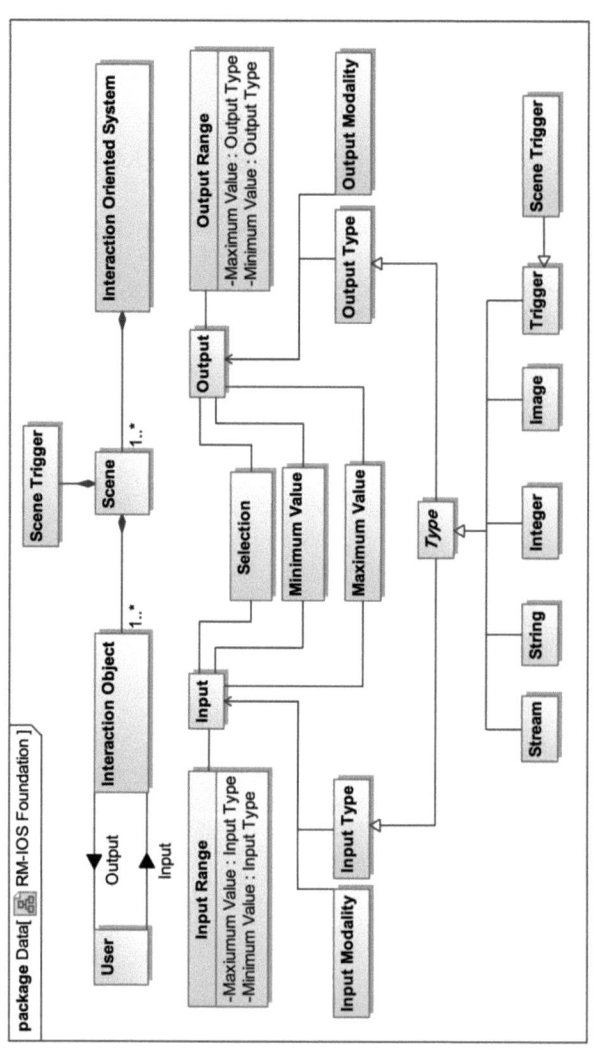

Figure 5.1: RM-IOS Foundation - UML Class Diagram

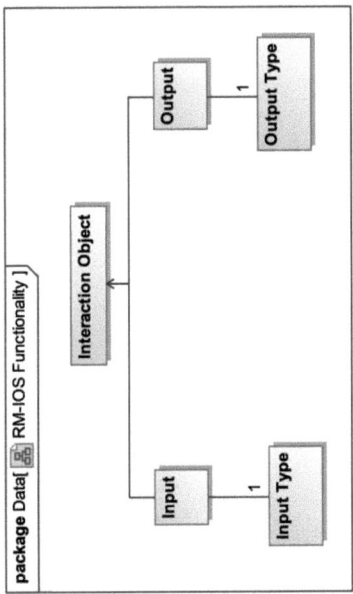

Figure 5.2: RM-IOS Functionality - UML Class Diagram

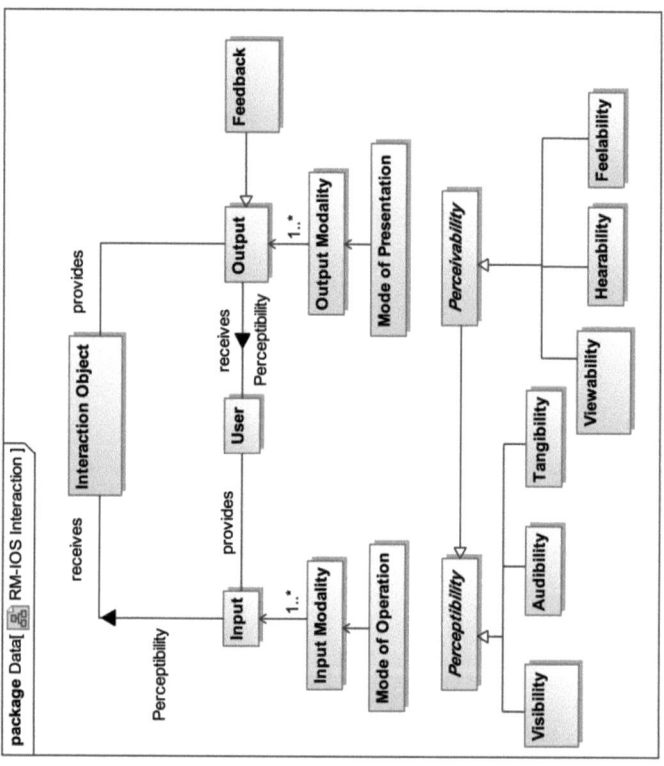

Figure 5.3: RM-IOS Interaction - UML Class Diagram

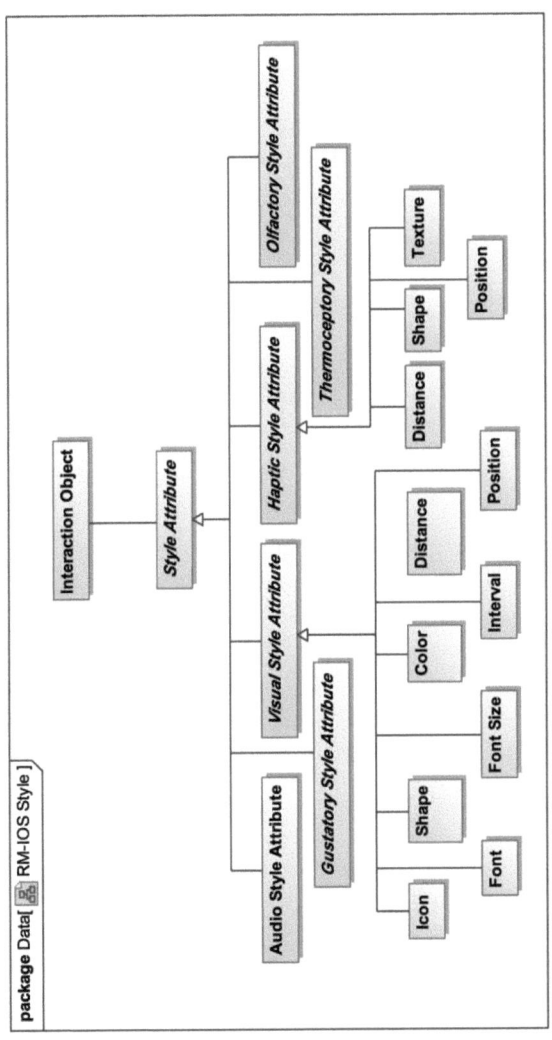

Figure 5.4: RM-IOS Style - UML Class Diagram

5.7 Conclusion

Shneiderman stipulates a holistic approach to the process of user interface development, acknowledging good usability as a systemic attribute of a system. The author of this thesis agrees with Shneiderman's recommendation for such a holistic approach, but feels it is important to keep in mind that a discipline as complex and interdisciplinary as the domain of user interface development must be subjected to a careful form of dissection in order to provide a clear policy of separation of concern, effectively bestowing experts from each discipline with the freedom to participate in the development process and avoiding a clash of responsibilities.

By providing a multiple-perspective based reference model the author feels that this goal has been reached satisfactorily in the *structural foundation* of the RM-IOS. Although the author also acknowledges that the style perspective, the one concerned with the aesthetic styling of the interaction oriented system, is - as a direct result of the author's own background in a technical engineering discipline - not as sophisticated as the other two perspectives. This, however, is not an impairment of the structural quality of the RM-IOS, only on the encompassing quality, which can be easily improved by extending this model. This is a task, though, that must be handed over to designers with a solid background in the respective fields, i.e. graphical, audio, haptical design.

The RM-IOS as presented here is to be understood as an initial proposal towards an encompassing, interdisciplinary, descriptive reference model in the domain of user interface development.

Chapter 6
Case Study

6.1 Case Study

As has been argued in section 4.2, no extensive empirical data about the Reference Model for Interaction Oriented Systems and its practicability could have been made available during the writing of this thesis. However, to present a proof of concept, a case study has been conducted which is being presented in this chapter. The goal of the case study is then the appraisal of whether the hypothesis underlying this thesis can be affirmed or must be dismissed.

Furthermore, by subjecting the Reference Model for Interaction Oriented Systems to a case study, however minimalistic, the soundness of the model can also be reviewed.[1].

A case study is a research methodology applied across a variety of disciplines, particularly in the disciplines of social science [Yin84]. A case study's goal is typically to "emphasize detailed contextual analysis of a limited number of events or conditions and their relationships" [Soy97].

Drawing upon the work of Robert E. Stakes [Sta95], Helen Simons [Sim80], and Robert K. Yin [Yin84] the following approach can be assumed as a standard approach in the field of case study research:

1. Determine and define the research questions
2. Select the cases and determine data gathering and analysis techniques

---

[1]In fact, the case study revealed certain short comings of the model, which had lead to modifications of the model and which will be divulged in the conclusion of this chapter (see section 6.6).

3. Prepare to collect the data

4. Collect data in the field

5. Evaluate and analyze the data

6. Prepare the report

Since this thesis constitutes a work in the engineering discipline, this just listed approach should be viewed accordingly. Taking this into consideration, the above listed approach can be realized as shown in the following list.

1. Determine and define the research questions:

    The research object in this case is the constructed Reference Model for Interaction Oriented Systems and the research question of interest will aim at confirming the propositions stipulated in the hypothesis. Thus, the research questions of interest this case study has to answer can be deduced from the hypothesis. The following questions are an excerpt from the hypothesis and constitute the research questions relevant for this case study.[2]

    - "Does the Reference Model for Interaction Oriented Systems support the descriptive modeling of an interaction oriented system while incorporating a policy of separation of concern regarding the different domains of skill and knowledge required during the user interface development process?"
    - "Does the Reference Model for Interaction Oriented Systems provide methodological ground for the analysis and evaluation of existing interaction solutions?"

    Both these questions are to be answered during the course of this case study and will be answered from the author's perspective in the conclusion of this chapter (see section 6.6).

2. Select the cases and determine data gathering and analysis techniques:

    The cases for this case study must be small enough to be handled during the course of this thesis, yet extensive enough to mirror the fundamental aspects and the nature of the Reference

---

[2]The statement of the hypothesis, whether the model "can be justified by what is known about successful interaction design and implementation endeavors" is not one that lends itself particularly well for the examination during a case study but rather must be answered through the quality of the development of the model. For that see chapter 4.

Model for Interaction Oriented Systems. Also, the author believes that it is suitable to put a contemporary case under the scrutiny of a case study as the Reference Model for Interaction Oriented Systems aims to contribute to ongoing design and development efforts in the field of user interaction. Subsequently, a system must be identified, that is not overly complex, yet imparts a sense of an actual real world situation. To fulfill these aspects, the author has decided to put the short messaging service applications of two contemporary smartphones, namely the Apple iPhone and the Palm Pre, to the examination of the case study. The data gathering and analysis techniques will be discussed further down.

3. Prepare to collect the data:

As opposed to case studies that possibly involve questioning and examining hundreds of people, the two objects of interest here were two smartphones. This reduced the usually necessary incentive for convincing the objects to participate in a case study to merely a loaded battery and a flick of the power switch – a most fortunate circumstance.

4. Collect data in the field:

The data collection consisted of examining the application on each smartphone in exactly the same way, under identical environmental circumstances, so as to produce identical quality of data for each device. The exact way of examining the applications will be described further down.

5. Evaluate and analyze the data:

The evaluation and analysis of the data will be presented in the conclusion of this chapter (see section 6.6).

6. Prepare the report:

The report encompasses all the findings of a case study and hence includes the answers to all the open questions above. The conclusion of this chapter (see section 6.6) will provide what is the equivalent to a case study report, by presenting the answers to the questions asked above and the conclusions drawn about the Reference Model for Interaction Oriented Systems.

While it might be argued, that a single case study can not provide sufficient evidence of, neither, affirmative nor negative kind, a proof of concept actually can be provided by a single case study, as its only intention is to show, that something can be made to work in accordance with its proclaimed intention. Another criticism might be that a case study about a model conducted by the creator of the model must contain a strong bias towards verification. The author acknowledges these possible criticisms, and relegates to the article of Flyvbjerg on the most common "Five Misunderstandings About Case-Study Research" [Fly06] in which he aptly illustrates, why even a single case study can be used for hypothesis testing, and a bias towards verification can not be confirmed:

> The case study contains no greater bias toward verification of the researcher's preconceived notions than other methods of inquiry. On the contrary, experience indicates that the case study contains a greater bias towards falsification of preconceived notions than toward verification.

Additionally, the words of Charles Darwin [Dar93] serve as an inspiration and reminder towards an important aspect during the conduction of a case study (or actually, the conduction of research in general) when he says:

> I had [...] during many years followed a golden rule, namely, that whenever a published fact, a new observation or thought came across me, which was opposed to my general results, to make a memorandum of it without fail and at once; for I had found by experience that such facts and thoughts were far more apt to escape from the memory than favorable ones.
>
> Owing to this habit, very few objections were raised against my views, which I had not at least noticed and attempted to answer. (p.123)

A fact which reminds of a phenomenon of the human nature given words to by Francis Bacon [Bac10] when he says that "It is the peculiar and perpetual error of the human understanding to be more moved and excited by affirmatives than negatives. (p. XLVI)".

Keeping all these aspects in mind the author has conducted the case study to the best of his knowledge and abilities and made notes of all unfavorable findings during the execution of the case study of all those aspects that did not seem to sit well with the intention of the Reference Model for Interaction Oriented Systems. These then actually did lead to the changing of the model in regards to those aspects (as already mentioned earlier) which is documented in the conclusion of this chapter (see section 6.6).

6.2 Case Study - Data Collection

This section starts with the presentation of the technical data of the case study, i.e. the devices used and the software version number of the apps at the point of the execution of the case study. Following that the data collected during the case study is being presented.

6.2.1 Technical Data

Object of the case study is actually the Reference Model for Interaction Oriented Systems, but in order to test it out it will be applied to the description and comparison of the short messaging service (SMS) app[3] on two different smartphones, namely, the Apple iPhone 3GS and the Palm Pre.

Both devices were first being sold in 2009 and thus, at the writing of this thesis, presented the state of the art in the smartphone industry. The Apple iPhone was chosen as it is possibly the most well known smartphone device, the Palm Pre was chosen as a device which was introduced to the market as a particularly user friendly device and one that introduced truly new ways of interacting with the phone when compared to other competitor's devices, i.e. the "swipe" gesture for managing the multiple apps running simultaneously on the device.

The Pre's operating system's version was webOS 1.4.1.1 and the iPhone's operating system's version was iOS 3.2 (7B367). The SMS app is part of the set of apps that come as part of the operating system on each device and thus has no version number of its own, at least none that can publicly be accessed and inspected. On the Apple iPhone the SMS app is named "Messages", on the Palm Pre the SMS app is named "Messaging". The operating system's version number, however, uniquely identifies the SMS app as well. The state of the app was in each case a certain scene in the SMS app in which the author had sent himself a message and replied to it once. A screenshot of that scene is being provided in the next section in figure 6.1. For quick reference the relevant data is being repeated in table 6.1.

6.2.2 Case Study Method

Whenever a case study is being conducted a certain method must be applied; whether that method is a well known and documented method or just a method created ad hoc by the person conducting

---

[3]Applications on smartphones are being called "apps", a term coined by Apple and now commonly used for applications across all contemporary smartphones.

Device:	Apple iPhone 3GS	Palm Pre
Operating System:	iOS 3.2 (7B367)	webOS 1.4.1.1
Inspected App:	Messages	Messaging

Table 6.1: Case Study - Technical Data

the case study and the approach. Whenever something is being done *some* method was being used. In this case the author attempted to create a method that was simplistic enough to 1) make it easily comprehensible and 2) be simple enough to let the Reference Model for Interaction Oriented Systems be in the main focus of the case study, and not the method itself. The result is an extremely minimalistic method that is also easily reproducible. This approach will be illustrated now.

This Case Study's Approach

During the case study the examination of one scene (in accordance with the definition of a scene from the Reference Model for Interaction Oriented Systems) on each device is being executed. The scenes will be from the SMS app on each device. The SMS app has been put as much as possible into the same state on each device in order to maximize the comparability of the scenes. That state has been created by the author sending himself a message and replying to it once thus generating a total of four messages in that conversation. The app was then closed, reopened, and the conversation entered again. In this state the scene has been inspected. A screenshot of each app can be seen in figure 6.1.

RM-IOS Elements Used From Each Perspective

That scene was then minimalistically described through each of the three perspectives offered by the Reference Model for Interaction Oriented Systems to inspect the crucial aspects of the inherent policy of separation of concern. At this point it is especially important to note that the entire case study was being conducted from *a user's point of view* on each of the apps, for access to the internal workings and data of the apps were not available to the author this was the only feasible approach. The result of this is that, for example, in the style perspective, no hexadecimal color code can be provided, as probably would have been used when such data is available during the development of an application or the inspection of its source code.

Case Study   CHAPTER 6

Figure 6.1: Screenshots of the Pre and iPhone for the Case Study

It was neither the author's intention, nor goal to describe the scene as completely as possible in terms of using as many model elements as possible but to focus on the core aspects of each perspective of the model. To realize this, the author selected the following elements of the model which were being used to describe the scene.

From the functionality perspective the following model elements were being used:

- Data Input
- Input Type
- Data Output
- Output Type

From the interaction perspective the following model elements were being used:

- Modality

Case Study CHAPTER 6

- Mode of Operation
- Mode of Presentation

From the style perspective the following model elements were being used:

- Color

Two of the characteristic elements of the interaction perspective, the elements of perceptibility and perceivability, were not being made part of this case study, as the inclusion of these two elements would have required a considerably more extensive case study which in turn would have shifted the focus away from the model and actually towards the examination of those two apps. Again, the object of interest during this case study is the Reference Model for Interaction Oriented Systems, not the inspected apps.

It must also be noted that the style perspective has received the least amount of attention during the conducting of the case study as in this case it was the most irrelevant perspective and partly also because the author does not have a background in the field of design and styling. This however does not impede the observation of whether the separation of styling relevant aspects from functionality and interaction related aspects can be achieved through the utilization of the Reference Model for Interaction Oriented Systems. It merely impedes the quantity and quality of the coverage of the styling relevant aspects.

Collection of the Data

The actual approach then was to inspect the scenes with the three questions defining for each perspective. Those were:

- From the functionality perspective: What input does the system need from the user and what output does the system provide to the user?
- From the interaction perspective: How does the user provide the input and how does the system provide the output?
- From the style perspective: What is the styling of the system's elements relevant to the input and output?

The devices were each inspected consecutively, in the same order: namely, first inspecting the interaction objects of the scene from the functionality perspective in regard to the interaction objects relevant to the *input*. Then inspecting the interaction objects of the scene from the functionality perspective in regard to the interaction objects relevant to the *output*. The same procedure was repeated from the interaction perspective and finally the style perspective, in each case examining the interaction objects relevant to the input, firstly, then the output, secondly.

This inspection was done by trying to activate each and every interaction object present in the scene[4] and evaluating every element for output it's providing. Figure 6.2 depicts a graphic of the structure of the data collected.

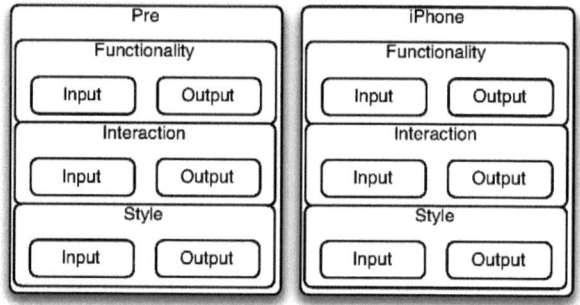

Figure 6.2: Structure of the Data Collected in the Case Study

During the inspection of the scene on each device no distinction was being made between interaction objects belonging to the actual app and interaction objects belonging to the operating system, i.e. interaction objects that are available across all apps because the operation system provides them. Firstly, these operating system interaction objects could only be identified during an analysis of the operating system by, for example, inspecting several applications for the presence of such elements, and secondly, this fact has absolutely no impairing effect on the outcome of the case study in this context.

To refer to the interaction objects across the different perspectives, the interaction objects inspected were being tagged by identifying strings which were used throughout the case study. pre_{in} in case

---

[4]For example by touching every element on the screen, as the screens on both devices are touch-sensitive and by inspecting the outside of the device for interaction objects in form of hardware buttons, switches, sliders and the like.

of the Pre's scene, with the index-letter 'i' indicating that it is an interaction object inspected during the examination of the input direction, while 'n' being the incremental index used to uniquely identify the interaction object. The identification tag $iphone_{on}$ would be used in case of the iPhone's scene, with the index-letter 'o' indicating that it is an interaction object inspected during the examination of the output direction, while 'n' being the incremental index used to uniquely identify the interaction object. This kind of identification is needed in order to be able to refer to one specific interaction object from each of the three perspectives.

To present the data collected during the execution of that examination in as concise a way as possible, it was formatted into tables for each of the three perspectives. These tables - all included on the next pages - are grouped by device first and then perspective second.

Once all these tables have been presented the case study continues to compare the scenes of each device with one another (see section 6.5) in a quantitative way. To reduce the complexity of that comparison, the data has been compressed by leaving out some of the data contained in the initial table of that perspective. The author provides his personal interpretation of that comparison at the end of the case study but this is merely to express his thoughts and demonstrate the ability of the Reference Model for Interaction Oriented Systems to provide an analyst with such data that can then be evaluated.

The reason for reducing the available data in the comparison is that the goal of the case study is to present the possibility of comparing scenes with one another which have been described (i.e. inspected) by using the Reference Model for Interaction Oriented Systems. It was not the goal of the case study to provide an extensive comparison of the two apps themselves. Such a comparison, however, would be very interesting indeed and could be done during the course of, for example, a bachelor thesis.

Summarizing it can be said, that this case study focuses on the description of scenes, which is done by presenting the collected data in tables and then compares the scenes quantitatively. This case study does not qualitatively analyze the scenes, as such an endeavor would require the expert input from interaction and style experts, neither of which the author claims to be one of.

6.2.3 Data Types in the Case Study

In the tables of the next sections the following data types appear:

- *Trigger*

- *String*
- *Expressive Text*
- *Contact*
- *Date*
- *Graphic*
- *Mark*

While the *Trigger* data type is a data type appearing in the Reference Model for Interaction Oriented Systems, the other types have been created for this case study and will be explained here. The reasons for the creation of those data types simply is that the "modeler"[5] felt these data types to adequately represent the data type occurring in the scene. Again, keeping in mind that the case study has been conducted from strictly an observer's or user's perspective (as opposed to a developer's perspective) the *actual* data type can not be known. But in this case the actual data type is irrelevant as it has no effect on the quality of the result of this case study. The only concern that must be satisfied here is that the modeler feels that he is using representative data types for the input and output between the system and the user. The above data types are now explained.

Trigger

Trigger is a data type from the reference model of interaction oriented systems. Whenever a term is being used in the course of a case study or project that is also being used by a model element in the reference model for interaction oriented system, that term should represent the model element from the Reference Model for Interaction Oriented Systems in order to avoid confusion. The *trigger* data type is here being used precisely as defined by the Reference Model for Interaction Oriented Systems.

String

The *string* is commonly used in information technology and especially programming languages to describe a linear sequence of symbols. That is precisely the meaning of the term here as well.

---

[5] Read: The author of this thesis.

Expressive Text

An *expressive text* is a composite data type comprising strings with the addition of emoticons being included in it. This happens on the Pre device when a message contains a certain combination of ASCII-symbols that are typically used in casual electronic communication to represent emoticons (see [Wor10]), i.e. to imply how the user feels or how a written text is meant to be interpreted (for example ironically or in jest)[6]. On the Pre, these emoticons are turned into little graphical icons, more vividly representing the emoticon as can be seen in the last two message on the screenshots of the scene inspected (see figure 6.1). In this case study the "expressive text" data type indicates this inclusion of graphical emoticons.

Contact

The data type *contact* is being used to imply that a contact from the user's address book is being referenced. This typically happens by displaying the contact's name, i.e. the name associated with the telephone-number the message came from.

Date

This data type has been introduced to express the representation of a date. There are several representations for a date, for example "September 27th 2010" or "27/9/2010". In either case, however, the information that is being conveyed refers to a certain date.

Graphic

A *graphic* is a visual representation of something typically other than a string or a number. A *graphic* can be iconic or, for example, a picture of something or someone. In the case of the Pre the contact is being represented by the picture that is saved in the contact's address book entry.

Mark

The data type *mark* is not so much a certain data type but rather implies that something is being marked, i.e. by changing the background color, as is the case when a message is being selected

---
[6]Typical emoticons include the smiley :-), the winking smiley ;-), or the sad smiley :-(.

for copying or forwarding in either case. While possibly a bit volatile in the nature of its definition, it still seems like a valid data type to be defined as it strongly conveys a certain information, for example that of selecting something.

6.3 Pre

6.3.1 Functionality

Input

Table 6.2 presents the data collected during the inspection of the Pre from the functionality perspective of the interaction objects relevant for the user to providing input to the system.

The first column lists the data input the user is able to provide to the app, i.e. all possible input the user can provide the system with in this particular scene. The second column lists the input type, that the data input is bound to, i.e. what input type is required by the data input to be provided by the user. The third column lists the unique identification each interaction object has been tagged with, the composition of which has been explained above.

DATA INPUT	INPUT TYPE	ID
Open app menu	Trigger	pre_{i1}
Show Contact Info	Trigger	pre_{i2}
Select Contact's Phone Number	Trigger	pre_{i3}
Forward / Forward via eMail / Copy / Delete	Trigger	pre_{i4}
Add Attachment	Trigger	pre_{i5}
Back to Conversation Overview	Trigger	pre_{i6}
Deactivate App	Trigger	pre_{i7}
Bring Up Dock Menu	Trigger	pre_{i8}
Message Text	Expressive Text	pre_{i9}
Send the Message	Trigger	pre_{i10}
Mute Telephone	Trigger	pre_{i11}
Stand-by Telephone	Trigger	pre_{i12}
Shutdown Menu	Trigger	pre_{i13}
Volume Control	Trigger	pre_{i14}
Take Screenshot	Trigger	pre_{i15}

Table 6.2: Pre - Data Input and Input Type (Functionality Input)

Case Study   CHAPTER 6

Output

Table 6.3 presents the data collected during the inspection of the Pre from the functionality perspective of the interaction objects relevant for the user to receiving output from the system. The first column lists the data output the system provides to the user in this scene. The second column lists the output type of the data output. The third column lists the unique identification each interaction object has been tagged with, the composition of which has been explained above.

DATA OUTPUT	OUTPUT TYPE	ID
App name	String	pre_{o1}
Contact to receive the message	Contact	pre_{o2}
Type of Message	String	pre_{o3}
Previously Sent Messages to this Contact	Expressive Text	pre_{o4}
Previously Received Messages from this Contact	Expressive Text	pre_{o5}
Time of Message	Date	pre_{o6}
Picture of Contact	Graphic	pre_{o7}
Hint-Text for Entering Text	String	pre_{o8}
Smiley Icon in Message Text	Graphic	pre_{o9}
Time	Date	pre_{o10}
Reception Strength	Graphic	pre_{o11}
Reception Type	Graphic	pre_{o12}
WiFi Rcpt. Strength	Graphic	pre_{o13}
Battery Status	Graphic	pre_{o14}

Table 6.3: Pre - Data Output and Output Type (Functionality Output)

6.3.2 Interaction

Input

Table 6.4 presents the data collected during the inspection of the Pre from the interaction perspective of the interaction objects relevant for the user to providing input to the system. The first column lists the modality of the information exchange. The second column lists the mode of operation. The third column lists the unique identification each interaction object has been tagged with which enables the elements of this table to be mapped against the elements of the table from the functionality perspective (see table 6.2).

MODALITY	MODE OF OPERATION	ID
Haptic	Virtual Button	pre_{i1}
Haptic	Virtual Button	pre_{i2}
Haptic	Virtual Button	pre_{i3}
Haptic	Virtual Button	pre_{i4}
Haptic	Virtual Button	pre_{i5}
Haptic	Gesture (right to left)	pre_{i6}
Haptic	Gesture (down to up)	pre_{i7}
Haptic	Gesture (full down to up)	pre_{i8}
Haptic	Keyboard	pre_{i9}
Haptic	Key (Enter Key)	pre_{i10}
Haptic	Virtual Button	pre_{i10}
Haptic	Slide switch	pre_{i11}
Haptic	Button	pre_{i12}
Haptic	Hold Down Button	pre_{i13}
Haptic	Rocker Button	pre_{i14}
Haptic	Key combination (Orange-, Sym-, and P key)	pre_{i15}

Table 6.4: Pre - Modality and Mode of Operation (Interaction Input)

Output

Table 6.5 presents the data collected during the inspection of the Pre from the interaction perspective of the interaction objects relevant for the user to receiving output from the system. The first column lists the modality of the information exchange. The second column lists the mode of presentation. The third column lists the unique identification each interaction object has been tagged with, which enables the elements of this table to be mapped against the elements of the table from the functionality perspective (see table 6.3).

MODALITY	MODE OF PRESENTATION	ID
Visual	String in Drop-Down Button	pre_{o1}
Visual	String in Headerpill	pre_{o2}
Visual	String in Drop-Down Button	pre_{o3}
Visual	Expressive Text Over Colored Background	pre_{o4}
Visual	Expressive Text Over Colored Background	pre_{o5}
Visual	String According to Date	pre_{o6}
Visual	Picture in Message	pre_{o7}
Visual	String in Empty Inputfield	pre_{o8}
Visual	Icon in Message-Text	pre_{o9}
Visual	String in Topbar	pre_{o10}
Visual	Graphic in Topbar	pre_{o11}
Visual	Graphic in Topbar	pre_{o12}
Visual	Graphic in Topbar	pre_{o13}
Visual	Graphic in Topbar	pre_{o14}

Table 6.5: Pre - Modality and Mode of Presentation (Interaction Output)

6.3.3 Style

Input

Table 6.6 presents the data collected during the inspection of the Pre from the style perspective of the interaction objects relevant for the user to providing input to the system. The first column lists the color of the interaction object. The second column lists the unique identification each interaction object has been tagged with which enables the elements of this table to be mapped against the elements of the table from the functionality and interaction perspective (see table 6.2 and table 6.4).

Output

Table 6.7 presents the data collected during the inspection of the Pre from the style perspective of the interaction objects relevant for the user to receiving output from the system. The first column lists the color of the information exchange. The second column lists the unique identification each

COLOR	ID
Light Grey	pre_{i1}
Light Grey Gradient	pre_{i2}
Black Expressive Text in Blue Bubble	pre_{i3}
Black String	pre_{i4}
Light Grey Gradient	pre_{i5}
Black String	pre_{i6}
(Picture)	pre_{i7}
Black	pre_{i8}
Light Grey	pre_{i9}
Black	pre_{i10}
Dark Grey	pre_{i10}
Black	pre_{i11}
Black	pre_{i12}
Black	pre_{i13}

Table 6.6: Pre (Style Input)

interaction object has been tagged with, which enables the elements of this table to be mapped against the elements of the table from the functionality and interaction perspective (see table 6.3 and table 6.5).

COLOR	ID
White	pre_{o1}
White	pre_{o2}
Grey	pre_{o3}
Black	pre_{o4}
Black	pre_{o5}
Grey	pre_{o6}
White Frame	pre_{o7}
Light Grey	pre_{o8}
Yellow	pre_{o9}
White	pre_{o10}
Light Grey / Dark Grey	pre_{o11}
White	pre_{o12}
White	pre_{o13}
White	pre_{o14}

Table 6.7: Pre (Style Output)

Case Study   CHAPTER 6

6.4 iPhone

6.4.1 Functionality

Input

Table 6.8 presents the data collected during the inspection of the iPhone from the functionality perspective of the interaction objects relevant for the user to providing input to the system.

The first column lists the data input the user is able to provide to the app, i.e. all possible input the user can provide the system with in this particular scene. The second column lists the input type, that the data input is bound to, i.e. what input type is required by the data input to be provided by the user. The third column lists the unique identification each interaction object has been tagged with, the composition of which has been explained above.

REQUIRED DATA INPUT	INPUT TYPE	ID
Back to Conversation Overview	Trigger	$iphone_{i1}$
Edit the Message History	Trigger	$iphone_{i2}$
Call Contact	Trigger	$iphone_{i3}$
Show Contact Info	Trigger	$iphone_{i4}$
Open Keyboard	Trigger	$iphone_{i5}$
Quit App / Return to Home Screen	Trigger	$iphone_{i6}$
Rotate Screen	Trigger	$iphone_{i7}$
Copy Message	Trigger	$iphone_{i8}$
Mute Telephone	Trigger	$iphone_{i9}$
Stand-by Telephone	Trigger	$iphone_{i10}$
Shutdown Menu	Trigger	$iphone_{i11}$
Volume Control	Trigger	$iphone_{i12}$
Take Screenshot	Trigger	$iphone_{i13}$

Table 6.8: iPhone - Data Input and Input Type (Functionality Input)

Output

Table 6.9 presents the data collected during the inspection of the iPhone from the functionality perspective of the interaction objects relevant for the user to receiving output from the system. The first column lists the data output the system provides to the user in this scene. The second column lists the output type of the data output. The third column lists the unique identification each interaction object has been tagged with, the composition of which has been explained above.

REQUIRED DATA OUTPUT	OUTPUT TYPE	ID
Name / Number of Contact	String	$iphone_{o1}$
Time of Message	Date	$iphone_{o2}$
Previously Sent Messages to this Contact	String	$iphone_{o3}$
Prev. Received Mess. from this Contact	String	$iphone_{o4}$
Message to be Copied	Mark	$iphone_{o5}$
Time	Date	$iphone_{o6}$
Reception Strength	Graphic	$iphone_{o7}$
Reception Type	Graphic	$iphone_{o8}$
WiFi Rcpt. Strength	Graphic	$iphone_{o9}$
Battery Status	Graphic	$iphone_{o10}$

Table 6.9: iPhone - Data Output and Output Type (Functionality Output)

6.4.2 Interaction

Input

Table 6.10 presents the data collected during the inspection of the iPhone from the interaction perspective of the interaction objects relevant for the user to providing input to the system. The first column lists the modality of the information exchange. The second column lists the mode of operation. The third column lists the unique identification each interaction object has been tagged with which enables the elements of this table to be mapped against the elements of the table from the functionality perspective (see table 6.8).

MODALITY	MODE OF OPERATION	ID
Haptic	Virtual Button	$iphone_{i1}$
Haptic	Virtual Button	$iphone_{i2}$
Haptic	Virtual Button	$iphone_{i3}$
Haptic	Virtual Button	$iphone_{i4}$
Haptic	Virtual Button	$iphone_{i5}$
Haptic	Button	$iphone_{i6}$
Equilibrioceptic	Rotate 90° to Side	$iphone_{i7}$
Haptic	Touch & Hold Message	$iphone_{i8}$
Haptic	Switch Button	$iphone_{i9}$
Haptic	Button	$iphone_{i10}$
Haptic	Hold Down Button	$iphone_{i11}$
Haptic	Rocker Button	$iphone_{i12}$
Haptic	Home-Button + Powerswitch	$iphone_{i13}$

Table 6.10: iPhone - Modality and Mode of Operation (Interaction Input)

Output

Table 6.11 presents the data collected during the inspection of the iPhone from the interaction perspective of the interaction objects relevant for the user to receiving output from the system. The first column lists the modality of the information exchange. The second column lists the mode of presentation. The third column lists the unique identification each interaction object has been tagged with, which enables the elements of this table to be mapped against the elements of the table from the functionality perspective (see table 6.9).

6.4.3 Style

Input

Table 6.12 presents the data collected during the inspection of the iPhone from the style perspective of the interaction objects relevant for the user to providing input to the system. The first column lists the color of the interaction object. The second column lists the unique identification each

MODALITY	MODE OF PRESENTATION	ID
Visual	String	$iphone_{o1}$
Visual	String	$iphone_{o2}$
Visual	String	$iphone_{o3}$
Visual	String	$iphone_{o4}$
Visual	Color Change	$iphone_{o5}$
Visual	String in Topbar	$iphone_{o6}$
Visual	Graphic in Topbar	$iphone_{o7}$
Visual	Graphic in Topbar	$iphone_{o8}$
Visual	Graphic in Topbar	$iphone_{o9}$
Visual	Graphic in Topbar	$iphone_{o10}$

Table 6.11: iPhone - Modality and Mode of Presentation (Interaction Output)

interaction object has been tagged with which enables the elements of this table to be mapped against the elements of the table from the functionality and interaction perspective (see table 6.8 and table 6.10).

Output

Table 6.13 presents the data collected during the inspection of the iPhone from the style perspective of the interaction objects relevant for the user to providing input to the system. The first column lists the data input of the of the information exchange. The second column lists the unique identification each interaction object has been tagged with, which enables the elements of this table to be mapped against the elements of the table from the functionality and interaction perspective (see table 6.9 and table 6.11).

6.5 Comparison

The Reference Model for Interaction Oriented Systems can be helpful in, both, the analysis and synthesis of interaction oriented systems. While the synthesis will not at all be part of this case study, the analysis comprises the description, evaluation, and comparison of interaction oriented

Case Study   CHAPTER 6

COLOR	ID
Greengrey	$iphone_{i1}$
Greengrey	$iphone_{i2}$
White	$iphone_{i3}$
White	$iphone_{i4}$
Blue Glossy Gradient	$iphone_{i5}$
Black/Grey	$iphone_{i6}$
-	$iphone_{i7}$
Black String	$iphone_{i8}$
Silver Metallic	$iphone_{i9}$
Silver Metallic	$iphone_{i10}$
Silver Metallic	$iphone_{i11}$

Table 6.12: iPhone (Style Input)

COLOR	ID
White	$iphone_{o1}$
Grey	$iphone_{o2}$
Black	$iphone_{o3}$
Black	$iphone_{o4}$
White/Grey/Blue	$iphone_{o5}$
Black	$iphone_{o6}$
Blue / Light Blue	$iphone_{o7}$
Blue	$iphone_{o8}$
Blue	$iphone_{o9}$
Adaptive Color	$iphone_{o10}$

Table 6.13: iPhone (Style Output)

system. The description of two scenes has been offered in the previous section, a very brief and personal evaluation will be offered as part of the conclusion of the case study (see 6.6). And the following section offers a comparison of the two scenes described above.

This comparison, also, is only a quantitative comparison while some qualitative assessment from the author's personal point of view is being provided in the conclusion of this thesis. While the benefit of a thorough comparison thus is not being provided in this thesis, the quantitative comparison offered here demonstrates how the Reference Model for Interaction Oriented Systems can be applied as a tool for that, as it allows a detailed presentation of scenes, separated into the domains of skills of functionality, interaction, and style related aspects.

6.5.1 Functionality

Input

Table 6.14 presents a selection of the data from the previous tables of the Pre's functionality input (table 6.2), and the iPhone's functionality input (table 6.8). The first entries up to the empty row of the table show those interaction objects on each device which provide the same functionality. The entries following after the empty row then present those interaction objects on each device, to which no interaction object with equivalent functionality exists on the other device.

This is to say, that the first entries of the table show the commonality of the two devices in terms of input required from the user, whereas the latter entries show the difference of the two devices in terms of input required from the user.

Table 6.14 then allows the direct comparison of the data input of the interaction objects.

Output

Table 6.15 presents a selection of the data from the previous tables of the Pre's functionality output (table 6.3), and the iPhone's functionality output (table 6.9). The first entries up to the empty row of the table show those interaction objects on each device which provide the same functionality. The entries following after the empty row then present those interaction objects on each device, to which no interaction object with equivalent functionality exists on the other device.

Case Study CHAPTER 6

DATA INPUT	ID	ID	DATA INPUT
Show Contact Info	pre_{i2}	$iphone_{i4}$	Show Contact Info
Fwd. (via eMail)/Copy/Delete	pre_{i4}	$iphone_{i8}$	Copy Message
Back to Con. Overview	pre_{i6}	$iphone_{i1}$	Back to Con. Overview
Deactivate App	pre_{i7}	$iphone_{i6}$	Quit App
Mute telephone	pre_{i11}	$iphone_{i9}$	Mute Telephone
Stand-by Telephone	pre_{i12}	$iphone_{i10}$	Stand-by Telephone
Shutdown Menu	pre_{i13}	$iphone_{i11}$	Shutdown Menu
Volume Control	pre_{i14}	$iphone_{i12}$	Volume Control
Take Screenshot	pre_{i15}	$iphone_{i13}$	Take Screenshot
Add Attachment	pre_{i5}	$iphone_{i5}$	Open Keyboard
Select Contact's Phone#	pre_{i3}	$iphone_{i7}$	Rotate Screen
Bring Up Dock Menu	pre_{i8}	$iphone_{i2}$	Edit the Msg. History
Message Expressive Text	pre_{i9}	$iphone_{i3}$	Call Contact
Open App Menu	pre_{i1}		
Send the Message	pre_{i10}		

Table 6.14: Pre - iPhone (Functionality Input)

This is to say, that the first entries of the table show the commonality of the two devices in terms of output presented to the user, whereas the latter entries show the difference of the two devices in terms of output presented to the user.

Table 6.15 then allows the direct comparison of the data output of the interaction objects.

6.5.2 Interaction

Input

Table 6.16 presents a selection of the data from the previous tables of the Pre's interaction input (table 6.4), and the iPhone's interaction input (table 6.10). The first entries up to the empty row of the table show those interaction objects on each device which provide the same functionality.

Case Study CHAPTER 6

DATA OUTPUT	ID	ID	DATA OUTPUT
Name/Number of Contact	pre_{o2}	$iphone_{o1}$	Name/Number of Contact
Prvsl. Sent Msgs.	pre_{o4}	$iphone_{o3}$	Prvsl. Sent Msgs.
Prvsl. Received Msgs.	pre_{o5}	$iphone_{o4}$	Prvsl. Received Msgs.
Time of Message	pre_{o6}	$iphone_{o2}$	Time of Message
Time	pre_{o10}	$iphone_{o6}$	Time
Reception Strength	pre_{o11}	$iphone_{o7}$	Reception Strength
Reception Type	pre_{o12}	$iphone_{o8}$	Reception Type
WiFi Rcpt. Strength	pre_{o13}	$iphone_{o9}$	WiFi Rcpt. Strength
Battery Status	pre_{o14}	$iphone_{o10}$	Battery Status
Type of Message	pre_{o3}	$iphone_{o5}$	Message to be Copied
Picture of Contact	pre_{o7}		
Hint String Input	pre_{o8}		
Smiley Icon in Message	pre_{o9}		
App Name	pre_{o1}		

Table 6.15: Pre - iPhone (Functionality Output)

The entries following after the empty row then present those interaction objects on each device, to which no interaction object with equivalent functionality exists on the other device.

This is to say, that the first entries of the table show the commonality of the two devices in terms of input required from the user, whereas the latter entries show the difference of the two devices in terms of input required from the user.

Table 6.16 then allows the direct comparison of the mode of operation of the interaction objects.

Output

Table 6.17 presents a selection of the data from the previous tables of the Pre's interaction output (table 6.5), and the iPhone's interaction output (table 6.11). The first entries up to the empty row of the table show those interaction objects on each device which provide the same functionality. The entries following after the empty row then present those interaction objects on each device, to which no interaction object with equivalent functionality exists on the other device.

MODE OF OPERATION	ID	ID	MODE OF OPERATION
Virtual Button	pre_{i2}	$iphone_{i4}$	Virtual Button
Virtual Button	pre_{i4}	$iphone_{i8}$	Touch&Hold
Gesture (right to left)	pre_{i6}	$iphone_{i1}$	Virtual Button
Gesture (down to up)	pre_{i7}	$iphone_{i6}$	Button
Slide Button	pre_{i11}	$iphone_{i9}$	Switch Button
Button	pre_{i12}	$iphone_{i10}$	Button
Rocker Switch	pre_{i13}	$iphone_{i11}$	Rocker Switch
Virtual Button	pre_{i5}	$iphone_{i5}$	Virtual Button
Virtual Button	pre_{i3}	$iphone_{i7}$	Rotate 90°
Gesture(full down to up)	pre_{i8}	$iphone_{i2}$	Virtual Button
Keyboard	pre_{i9}	$iphone_{i3}$	Virtual Button
Virtual Button	pre_{i1}		
Key (Enter Key)	pre_{i10}		
Virtual Button	pre_{i10}		

Table 6.16: Pre - iPhone (Interaction Input)

This is to say, that the first entries of the table show the commonality of the two devices in terms of output presented to the user, whereas the latter entries show the difference of the two devices in terms of output presented to the user.

Table 6.17 then allows the direct comparison of the mode of operation of the interaction objects.

6.5.3 Style

6.5.4 Input

Table 6.18 presents a selection of the data from the previous tables of the Pre's style input (table 6.6), and the iPhone's style input (table 6.12). The first entries up to the empty row of the table show those interaction objects on each device which provide the same functionality. The entries following after the empty row then present those interaction objects on each device, to which no interaction object with equivalent functionality exists on the other device.

MODE OF PRES.	ID	ID	MODE OF PRES.
String in Headerpill	pre_{o2}	$iphone_{o1}$	String in Headerbox
Expressive Text Over Col. BG	pre_{o4}	$iphone_{o3}$	String Over Colored BG
Expressive Text Over Col. BG	pre_{o5}	$iphone_{o4}$	String Over Colored BG
String	pre_{o6}	$iphone_{o2}$	String
String	pre_{o10}	$iphone_{o6}$	String
Graphic in Topbar	pre_{o11}	$iphone_{o7}$	Graphic in Topbar
Graphic in Topbar	pre_{o12}	$iphone_{o8}$	Graphic in Topbar
Graphic in Topbar	pre_{o13}	$iphone_{o9}$	Graphic in Topbar
Graphic in Topbar	pre_{o14}	$iphone_{o10}$	Graphic in Topbar
String in Drop-Down Button	pre_{o3}	$iphone_{o5}$	Color Change
Picture in Message	pre_{o7}		
String in Empty Textfield	pre_{o8}		
Icon in Message Text	pre_{o9}		
String in Drop-Down Button	pre_{o1}		

Table 6.17: Pre - iPhone (Interaction Output)

This is to say, that the first entries of the table show the commonality of the two devices in terms of input required from the user, whereas the latter entries show the difference of the two devices in terms of input required from the user.

Table 6.18 then allows the direct comparison of the color of the interaction objects.

Output

Table 6.19 presents a selection of the data from the previous tables of the Pre's style output (table 6.7), and the iPhone's style output (table 6.13). The first entries up to the empty row of the table show those interaction objects on each device which provide the same functionality. The entries following after the empty row then present those interaction objects on each device, to which no interaction object with equivalent functionality exists on the other device.

COLOR	ID	ID	COLOR
Light Grey Gradient	pre_{i2}	$iphone_{i4}$	White
Black String	pre_{i4}	$iphone_{i8}$	Black String
Black String	pre_{i6}	$iphone_{i1}$	Greengrey
Black	pre_{i11}	$iphone_{i9}$	Silver Metallic
Black	pre_{i12}	$iphone_{i10}$	Silver Metallic
Black	pre_{i13}	$iphone_{i11}$	Silver Metallic
Light Grey Gradient	pre_{i5}	$iphone_{i5}$	Blue Glossy Gradient
(Picture)	pre_{i7}	$iphone_{i3}$	White
Black	pre_{i8}	$iphone_{i2}$	Greengrey
Light Grey	pre_{i9}	$iphone_{i6}$	Black/Grey
Light Grey	pre_{i1}		
Black	pre_{i10}		
Dark Grey	pre_{i10}		
Black String in Blue Bubble	pre_{i3}		
		$iphone_{i7}$	-

Table 6.18: Pre - iPhone (Style Input)

This is to say, that the first entries of the table show the commonality of the two devices in terms of output presented to the user, whereas the latter entries show the difference of the two devices in terms of output presented to the user.

Table 6.19 then allows the direct comparison of the color of the interaction objects.

COLOR	ID	ID	COLOR
White	pre_{o2}	$iphone_{o1}$	White
Black	pre_{o4}	$iphone_{o3}$	Black
Black	pre_{o5}	$iphone_{o4}$	Black
Grey	pre_{o6}	$iphone_{o2}$	Grey
White	pre_{o10}	$iphone_{o6}$	Black
Light Grey / Dark Grey	pre_{o11}	$iphone_{o7}$	Blue / Light Blue
White	pre_{o12}	$iphone_{o8}$	Blue
White	pre_{o13}	$iphone_{o9}$	Blue
White	pre_{o14}	$iphone_{o10}$	Adaptive Color
Grey	pre_{o3}	$iphone_{o5}$	White/Grey/Blue
White Frame	pre_{o7}		
Light Grey	pre_{o8}		
Yellow	pre_{o9}		
White	pre_{o1}		

Table 6.19: Pre - iPhone (Style Output)

6.6 Conclusion

The execution of the case study served three purposes. The first purpose was to demonstrate a proof of concept that the Reference Model for Interaction Oriented Systems can actually be applied in a practical way. The second purpose, akin to the first, was to demonstrate, that the Reference Model for Interaction Oriented Systems fulfills the requirements defined by the hypothesis. The third purpose was to critically examine the Reference Model for Interaction Oriented Systems and generate informative feedback on its structure and model elements, effectively helping during the

Case Study CHAPTER 6

creation and leading to the improvement of the Reference Model for Interaction Oriented Systems. That feedback will be discussed in the following subsection. The other two aspects will follow afterwards.

6.6.1 Feedback for the Reference Model for Interaction Oriented Systems

This subsection presents elements that were created as a direct result of the conduction of the case study. During the case study some fundamental shortcomings of the model were being realized and subsequently fixed. This demonstrates that the case study added a much needed practical view on the Reference Model for Interaction Oriented Systems which, up to that point, had been created based on theoretical and analytical grounds alone.

The elements refined or added to the Reference Model for Interaction Oriented Systems caused by discoveries during the case study are being listed here. It should demonstrate, both, that creating a model that aims to be of practical use from only a theoretical perspective can fall short of its intention, and that the case study has been more than only a means to show case the Reference Model for Interaction Oriented Systems but was actually a vital part in the reiterative process of creating the model.

Scene

An absolutely crucial result of the case study in terms of the refinement of the Reference Model for Interaction Oriented Systems was the addition of the "scene" element (and the "scene trigger" subsequently). The scene was not part of the model at the beginning of the execution of the case study, albeit the case study was being conducted in such a manner that already adhered to the *concept* of the scene, namely inspecting all interaction elements available in that particular "snapshot" of the application and stopping whenever the "snapshot" changed noticeably. After a while the question crystallized as to what exactly constitutes and justifies the limit of the inspection during this case study. Pondering this question it became clear that it had to be possible to describe a certain "state" of an application in order to be able to provide a description of the interaction objects in that "state". This eventually lead to the concept of the scene (see page 72) and subsequently to the creation of the scene trigger, which was stringently necessary after the scene element was created. The scene then also enabled the precise definition of an interaction oriented system (see page 71) which effectively provided a fundamentally required completion of the model.

Mode of Operation and Mode of Presentation

At the initial execution of the case study, the Reference Model for Interaction Oriented Systems did not include the elements "Mode of Operation" and "Mode of Presentation". During the case study then, when trying to describe the inspected interaction objects of the scene from the interaction perspective, it became immediately obvious that the model was incomplete for the purpose of producing a description of practical value of an interaction oriented system. Describing only the modality of an interaction object seemed to stop too early regarding the specific "feel" of an interaction object, as obviously an interaction object that is merely described as being a visual one still leaves a huge array of possibilities as to exactly how that interaction object appears.

This blatantly apparent shortcoming of the descriptive power of the Reference Model for Interaction Oriented Systems was corrected by introducing the two model elements "Mode of Operation" and "Mode of Presentation" which now enabled the modeler to precisely capture, not only the generic modality of an interaction object, but also the specificity of an interaction object's "interactiveness" with the user.

Equilibrioceptic Interaction

The element of equilibrioceptic interaction was added to the model during the discovery of the possibility to rotate the iPhone in order to rotate the screen. While several modalities are being included as stubs (for example the gustatory modality), this modality may have escaped that collection had it not been for the actual occurence in the iPhone's scene.

Minimum Value and Maximum Value

Another, although indirect, result of the case study was the moving of the model elements "Minimum Value" and "Maximum Value" from the functionality perspective, where they were initially contained, into the foundation. As it initially appeared that those two aspects were purely functionality related that view had to be corrected as it was realized that the fact that a minimum and maximum value are present very much influences the choices made regarding the interaction and style of that element. Should an interaction object be restricted by either or both, a minimum or maximum value this had to be made available to all three perspectives. Good examples of the different interaction with a restricted input value and an unrestricted input value are for example a round turning knob and a slider. Where the round turning knob could be used to adjust an unrestricted value, the slider inherently has a minimum (the lowest end) and a maximum (the highest end) value it restricts the user to.

The situation that triggered this realization was the inspection of the "message type" virtual button on the Pre, where a list of message types is being presented. Pondering the presentation of this list caused the realization that an existing minimum and maximum value (or the non-existence thereof respectively) definitely influences this decision. As the minimum and maximum value where then moved into the foundation, the selection element followed, as the selection element just describes the coexistence of, both, a minimum and maximum value.

6.7 Evaluation of the Case Study

The evaluation of the case study is being broken up into two parts. The first part concentrates on the two scenes and by providing some evaluating thoughts demonstrates how the Reference Model for Interaction Oriented Systems opens up the space for the analysis of interaction oriented systems. That part, however, does not claim to provide a particularly deep and insightful evaluation but merely presents the author's personal thoughts on the two scenes. The second part concentrates on the evaluation of the Reference Model for Interaction Oriented Systems after the case study as a practical appliance of the model and proof of concept has been concluded.

6.7.1 Evaluation in Regard to the Inspected Scenes

This is a rudimentary evaluation of the data collected about the scenes during the case study that was being conducted as part of this thesis. Its purpose is to merely demonstrate the fact that such an evaluation can be done based on the description of an interaction oriented systems by using the model elements provided by the Reference Model for Interaction Oriented Systems.

Comparison of the Pre's and iPhone's Scene

When comparing the two scenes with one another the following observations can be made. The Pre provides a greater amount of functionality which can be easily recognized through the amount of input and output functionality available to the user as presented by tables 6.2, 6.3, 6.8, and 6.9. This can be argued as, both, a positive or negative aspect of the Pre's app. The positive point of view would argue, that the app is providing more functionality to the user, the negative point of view would argue, that the iPhone focuses on the essential and truly important functionality of such an app. Only an extensive field study including a statistically relevant number of participating test users could give substance to either claim. The author is inclined to see this as a positive aspect of the Pre's app. As for example the inclusion of little graphical emoticons in the message text add an increased element of personality to the message text absent from the iPhone's presentation of the messages. And the absence of ability to send an attachment with a message seems quite inexcusable for a device like the iPhone.

A pivotal difference, however, is the variety of modes of operations on each device (see tables 6.4 and 6.10). With the exception of the equilibrioceptic input of rotating the device on the iPhone, all other modes of operation consist of virtual or real buttons. Whereas the Pre adds a variety of gestures to the "mode of operation"-set, along with the coexistence of real keys on the keyboard and virtual buttons on the interface. The author believes that, while both these modes of operation add an element of convenience and increased accessibility to the functionality of the app when known well, they probably are a source of confusion for the novice user of the device. Here, the need of an instructive tutorial or usually dreaded manual becomes apparent, a circumstance the iPhone successfully circumvents by reducing the mode of operations to a very homogenous array of possibilities.

A negative aspect that was spotted during the case study was the discovery of lack of feedback on one of the Pre's interaction objects. This aspect is actually not included in the tables of the case study, as "feedback" was not made a column in the tables (as all elements except for one provided feedback it would have been a rather unimpressive column and the lack of feedback on that one element is being covered here now). The element in question is the interaction object pre_{i1}, the virtual button to open the app menu. Which when touched (activated) does not give any sort of feedback that this activation has been registered by the app. All other interaction objects provide this feedback by changing their color while being touched, but this element does nothing and the user just has to wait the moment to find out whether he managed to hit the especially small virtual button in the top left corner of the screen. During moments of increased background activity – which can happen quite often on the Pre as it allows for the user to have several apps running simultaneously (a feature desperately missing on the iPhone) – it can take up to a few seconds before the actual result of the activating of that interaction object appears, namely, the showing of the app menu. In these situations the lack of feedback is particularly bothersome as not seeing the app menu showing up right away typically leads the user (including the author of this thesis) to the repeated touching of that virtual button which then, once the device processes the queued up input, results in the quick succession of opening, closing, opening, and closing of the app menu. This is such a ridiculous oversight on the side of Palm that the author can only speculate that it must have simply been missed during the testing of the device. Providing feedback on the user's interaction with the system is one of the most fundamental and simplistic rules of good interface design – and not without reason one of Shneiderman's "golden rules". The positive aspect of this usability blooper by Palm, however, is that it demonstrates the Reference Model for Interaction Oriented Systems' ability to discover the aspect of provided feedback (or lack thereof) quite aptly. The author is grateful to the inattentive user-interface tester in Palm's developer team for this possibility.

And speaking of app menus: An interesting aspect that the case study exposed was the lack of an app menu in the iPhone's app. This signifies a difference in philosophy regarding apps on Palm's and Apple's side. While the app in the Pre with its app menu works similar to an application on a desktop computer, by providing a menu in which, for example, the preferences can be set, the app in the iPhone works more like a small, completely specialized and flat[7] application. The immediate result of this different approach is that the iPhone does not have to deal with the layout of pull-down menu structures and the clutter on the screen caused by this. While certainly a change to the approach how a user interacts with an application, the author believes that the iPhone's approach here seems more appropriate to the environment of contemporary smartphones.

A peculiar fact, then, was the discovery of the user actually not being able to enter any message text at the iPhone's scene that was being inspected. As the iPhone is a purely "virtual keyboard" device (whereas the Pre provides a real keyboard that can be slid out from the device) and at the scene no virtual keyboard is being presented, it is impossible for the user to enter text. Apple solves this in a clever way by providing a button at the bottom of the screen that looks like a textfield and another graphic that looks like a button to the right of it (see figure 6.1). This actually is not a textfield, however. Rather the whole area is a virtual button that when tapped causes the virtual keyboard to slide up from the bottom of the screen now enabling the user to enter text. The cleverness of this method is the fact that the commonly known behavior of a textfield is to blink a text-cursor when the textfield is ready to receive input. As the textfield on the iPhone does not show such a blinking cursor, the user wants to "activate" the textfield and taps into it, effectively clicking on a virtual button in disguise. The following effect of the virtual keyboard appearing is not part of the

---

[7] In terms of uncomplex and accessible.

scene that was being inspected, however, and thus can only be included here. The author believes that it very nicely shows the analytical power provided by using the Reference Model for Interaction Oriented Systems.

Another difference between the iPhone's and the Pre's app in the inspected scene is that the iPhone clearly indicates where the user can navigate "back" to, by including the description in the virtual button (see interaction object $iphone_{i1}$). The equivalent functionality of navigating back to the conversation overview is triggered in the Pre's app by the globally available gesture "right to left" (see interaction object pre_{i6}). This, however, does not provide the user with a sense of exactly where he can and will navigate "back" to. A minor drawback only, but one discovered during the description of the scene by utilizing the Reference Model for Interaction Oriented Systems and thus a drawback worth mentioning.

This concludes the author's brief evaluation of the two scenes described by using the Reference Model for Interaction Oriented Systems. Obviously a more qualified evaluation would be possible, but this realization is exactly the purpose of this evaluation: to demonstrate the Reference Model for Interaction Oriented Systems' ability to provide methodological ground for the analysis and evaluation of existing interaction solutions.

6.7.2 Evaluation in Regard to the RM-IOS

The research questions underlying the case study were presented in the beginning of this chapter (see page 115) and this evaluation must now answer to them.

Policy of Separation of Concern

The first research question, whether the Reference Model for Interaction Oriented Systems supports the descriptive modeling of an interaction oriented system while incorporating a policy of separation of concern regarding the different domains of skill and knowledge required during the user interface development process can be answered affirmatively: The case study has shown that the appliance of the Reference Model for Interaction Oriented Systems during the description of an interaction oriented system is feasible and produces a description of practical value.

The policy of separation of concern is inherent to the structure of the Reference Model for Interaction Oriented Systems and its completeness in regard to the user interface development process has already been confirmed during the development of the model (see chapter 4). However, that confirmation was from a theoretical point of view while the case study now provided the confirmation from a practical point of view. Inspecting the tables offered in the preceding section of this chapter a clearly realized policy of separation of concern can be observed as the tables presenting the data collected during the inspection of the scene from each perspective primly observes the distinctly different domains of skill each perspective in the reference model for interaction oriented system represents.

Another important aspect of a successful policy of separation of concern is the independence of each perspective from one another. The case study has shown that the Reference Model for Interaction Oriented Systems allows for the description of an interaction oriented system from three perspectives independently from one another.

The combination of these two just described aspects constitutes a successful realization of a policy of separation of concern by the Reference Model for Interaction Oriented Systems. This policy of separation of concern was one of the requirements stated in the hypothesis that the Reference Model for Interaction Oriented Systems verifiably fulfills.

Provision of Methodological Ground

The second research question, whether the Reference Model for Interaction Oriented Systems provides methodological ground for the analysis and evaluation of existing interaction solutions can also be answered affirmatively: The case study has shown that the description of an interaction oriented system through the model elements provided by the Reference Model for Interaction Oriented Systems resulted in a detailed, exposing view on the described interaction oriented system.

This view then allowed for further analysis and evaluation of the described system which has been provided in a rudimentary form in subsection 6.7.1.

The humble quality of the analysis and evaluation given there is only founded in the humble abilities of the author to provide such an analysis and evaluation for which expert knowledge in the respective fields is required. The fact that such analysis and evaluation was being enabled by the use of the Reference Model for Interaction Oriented Systems to describe an interaction oriented system, however, remains untouched by just acknowledged curtailment.

Chapter 7
Conclusion

This chapter presents the contributions made by this thesis and offers a suggestion of potential future works that may extend this thesis or build on top of it.

7.1 Summary of Contributions

This book's contribution is mainly made to the field of engineering of human computer interaction. The Reference Model for Interaction Oriented Systems introduced here enables the interdisciplinary collaboration of three important areas of skill on a user interface development project, namely, the discipline of software development, the discipline of human computer interaction design, and the related disciplines of artistic design. This collaboration is being enabled by realizing a policy of separation of concern in the structure of the model, thus, allowing the expertise from those disciplines to be brought together while drawing the border lines of responsibility for each.

The contribution of this thesis can then be viewed from two different perspectives:

1. From the analytical perspective
2. From the synthetical perspective

The following sections will present the contributions made by this thesis in regard to these two perspectives.

7.1.1 Contributions - From the Analytical Perspective

The analytical perspective of software development comprises the description, comparison, verification, and evaluation of systems. The analytical perspective is one on an *existing* system which is the object of interest.

Description

In the domain of software development a description of a system is a model of the system that serves the purpose of providing an objective depiction of the system. In order for a description to be of practical value, it must be anchored in a vocabulary commonly accessible by all stakeholders involved. Such a vocabulary is the necessary premise to avoid ambiguities and provide mental models of the concepts contained within it. The Reference Model for Interaction Oriented Systems provides such a vocabulary for the description of interaction oriented systems from three perspectives which can be conjoined in the element of the interaction object.

Comparison

Two or more systems can be compared with one another, however, the basis for a meaningful comparison is an objective and uniform description. As just previously shown, the Reference Model for Interaction Oriented Systems provides the means for producing such a description, and thus, in consequence provides the basis for the comparison of two or more interaction oriented systems in those aspects captured by the Reference Model for Interaction Oriented Systems.

Verification

Verification of a system is a means to ensure that the requirements described in a specification of a system are being met by the system and is a fundamentally important aspect in the completion, i.e. delivery and acceptance, of a system. The Reference Model for Interaction Oriented Systems can be used as a tool for verification by checking the system for the fulfillment described through elements of the Reference Model for Interaction Oriented Systems.

Evaluation

Evaluation is the normative revision of a system. When a system has been described, the Reference Model for Interaction Oriented Systems provides a framework for an evaluation to be drawn from the description.

7.1.2 Contributions - From the Synthetical Perspective

The synthetical perspective of software development comprises the specification and modeling for the purpose of building of a system. The synthetical perspective is one on a system S that does *not yet exist*. Effectively saying, that S merely exists in the conception of the stakeholders and thus must be externalized appropriately.

Specification

Specification is a certain kind of description, namely, a binding description of a system yet to be built that is typically set during the early stages of the development cycle and which allows the customer to express his wants and needs for the system, and allows the developer to estimate the time and effort needed to be put into the development of such a system, and in turn give an estimation of the cost to be expected. The reference model for interaction oriented system provides an interdisciplinary vocabulary for the realization of such a specification.

7.1.3 Modeling

The modeling of a system is a process that is prevalent throughout both stages of system development, i.e. the stages of analysis and the stages of synthesis. The reference model for interaction oriented system provides a modeling framework for modeling a system which allows for the reduction of complexity in regard to that particular perspective and thus results in structural clarity helpful for the description and perception of the modeled interaction oriented system.

Furthermore, the Reference Model for Interaction Oriented Systems includes certain aspects of human computer interaction in a structured manner, bringing some implicit aspects from the interpretation of usability guidelines to the explicit realm of modeling. By identifying some elements which do not have to be surrendered to merely the talent in human computer interaction of the respective developers involved in the development process the Reference Model for Interaction Oriented Systems provides a way to repeat the successful usability and interaction design of certain systems.

Also, through the tripartite nature of the Reference Model for Interaction Oriented Systems, the model provides a gateway of model-based communication between those experts from the domains of functionality, interaction, and style.

7.1.4 Internal Validation

To validate the Reference Model for Interaction Oriented Systems proposed in this thesis it must be analytically assessed against a set of selected criteria. Those criteria are given in the hypothesis and are the requirements of this model. This section inspects the fulfillment of those requirements. The requirements were:

1. Mirroring the separated domains of skill, knowledge, and expertise required to cope with the needs of successful interaction design and implementation.

2. Covering the many aspects to be dealt with in successful interaction design and implementation.

3. Providing methodological ground for analysis and evaluation of existing interaction solutions.

4. Providing the basis for proper organization of development teams for interaction design and implementation.

5. It can be justified by what is known about successful interaction design and implementation endeavors.

These points will now be discussed from a rational point of view in an attempt to provide an internal validation of the fulfillment of these goals.

1. The Reference Model for Interaction Oriented Systems incorporates a tripartite structure that reflects the identified domains of skill, knowledge, and expertise as fundamental perspectives on contemporary interaction oriented system. These three domains and the segmentation of the model into these have been built on the identification of aspects relevant in contemporary interaction oriented system, the identifying of associational attributes in these aspects, and

the resulting domains of skill and knowledge realizable by dividing the whole of aspects at the least connected borders (see chapter 4).

2. The Reference Model for Interaction Oriented Systems provides an extensive vocabulary for the modeling of interaction oriented systems. These aspects have been gathered by identifying the core concepts present in the guides and recommendations of accredited experts in the field of human computer interaction and usability. By making these aspects readily available they are being raised into the field of awareness of those involved in, both, the synthetic processes, as well as the analytical processes of interaction oriented systems.

3. In the domain of software development a methodology is a framework for providing structured and reproducible processes to analyzing or synthesizing a system. By offering the means to break a system down into its elements (in regard to the domain of functionality, interaction, and style) the perceived complexity of a system can be reduced and the system can be approached from those perspectives. This, in theory, provides methodological ground for the analysis and evaluation of interaction solutions. (The case study offers a much more tangible external validation of this aspect.)

4. Akin to the preceding point, the disassembling of a system in a well defined and structured way based on a policy of separation of concerns which in turn has been deduced from the involved areas of expertise and knowledge, offers the possibility to organize development teams accordingly. The Reference Model for Interaction Oriented Systems provides the necessary perspective based approach for realizing such organization by incorporating a perspective based structure.

5. The analytical process of developing the Reference Model for Interaction Oriented Systems has been anchored in the best practice advice and guides offered by accredited usability experts, exemplary, on the "eight golden rules of user interface design" by Shneiderman. This ensures the inclusion of currently available knowledge about successful interaction design and implementation endeavors.

7.1.5 External Validation

The external validation of the goals set in the hypothesis for the Reference Model for Interaction Oriented Systems has been provided in the case study conducted for this thesis (see chapter 6). The external validation had to be restricted to certain goals, however, as some goals, especially those regarding the usefulness of the Reference Model for Interaction Oriented Systems for the synthesis of interaction oriented systems could not have been carried out in a significantly meaningful way during the course of this thesis. The empirical justification for the potential contribution of the Reference Model for Interaction Oriented Systems in regard to the synthesis of interaction oriented systems is a matter outside the scope of this thesis and could only be provided by actually employing the model in follow up projects. However, some aspects have been successfully backed by the findings of the case study and those will be presented here. The following list refers to the points listed above which are the goals formulated in the hypothesis.

1. The conduction of the case study has shown that the Reference Model for Interaction Oriented Systems provides a practical policy of separation of concern which realizes the required realization of such a policy as set out in the hypothesis.

2. The conduction of the case study has shown that the scenes of the systems that were being subjected to the description produced by the application of the Reference Model for Interaction Oriented Systems covered many of the aspects of those systems in regard to the three perspectives incorporated by the model. The descriptions presented in section 6.3 and following offer a description of the system by systematically presenting the aspects of the system from each of the three perspectives.

3. As briefly covered in the case study, the initial description produced during the case study provided a methodological ground for the following evaluation of the two scenes. The briefness of the evaluation is only owed to the fact that the author of this thesis can not provide a more in-depth evaluation, but it was demonstrated that an extensive evaluation could have been provided, given the required expertise for such an evaluation had been available.

4. This aspect could not have been covered during the conduction of the case study for this thesis, as it would have required the inclusion of a large development team in order to verify this point. Thus, only the internal validation, i.e. the analytically based assumption of this aspect, can be given (see above).

5. This aspect, too, is an aspect that relies rather on an internal validation than an external one, and so this point has been validated above by showing that the reference model for interaction

oriented system is based on the knowledge of accredited user interface engineering experts and their contemporary advice and guidance.

The reasoning behind these statements can be found in the conclusion of the case study in section 6.6.

7.2 Future Work in Prospect

Part of the quality of a scientific contribution as being made by such a thesis here can be found in the preceding work it builds on and the future work it leads to. The preceding work this thesis is built upon has been presented partly in chapter 2 and mostly in chapter 3. This section now aims to provide possible future work that could be build on top of this thesis.

- The synthesis of an interaction oriented system based on the reference model for interaction oriented system is not part of this thesis but would be an interesting prospect. It is thinkable for a development methodology to be anchored in the reference model for interaction oriented system, utilizing its descriptive power during the course of initial system conception, description, and possibly specification. A simple proof of concept of this could be provided during the course of a master thesis.

- It would be an interesting verification of and promising possibility regarding the extension of the Reference Model for Interaction Oriented Systems to try to describe a guideline available to system developers such as for example Apple's human interface guideline [Inc06] with the vocabulary of the Reference Model for Interaction Oriented Systems. Such a project would verify the expressive power of the Reference Model for Interaction Oriented Systems and detect shortcomings and needs for extensions in a structured and analytical way.

- As just mentioned, the reference model for interaction oriented system should be extended, especially the style perspective, as that one is clearly the weakest of the three perspectives, owed to the author's lack of expertise in the area of artistic design. A sensible first approach here seems to be the cooperation with someone with appropriate knowledge in the field of artistic design and try to work that knowledge into the style perspective of the Reference Model for Interaction Oriented Systems.

- Information science is a science of models and a plethora of models exist for this discipline. A very interesting future work would be the investigation of the possibility of combining the Reference Model for Interaction Oriented Systems with other models prevalent in the domain of software development for human computer interaction. Explicit examples could be the conjunction of the Reference Model for Interaction Oriented Systems with the GOMS model, or UML activity diagrams as those are two examples of models covering completely different aspects of modeling in the domain of software development for human computer interaction.

- A possible future work of grand proportion would be the implementation of an integrated developing environment (IDE) based on the principles of model driven development (MDD) with the reference model of interaction oriented systems as a basis. This would require considerable resources in, both, time and expertise needed.

- An obvious future work would be the extension of the case study presented here to the description of not only two scenes of an app, but two complete apps. The feedback to be had from such an extensive case study should provide valuable inspiration to the further improvement of the Reference Model for Interaction Oriented Systems.

Reviewing the possible future work with and for the Reference Model for Interaction Oriented Systems just given illustrates the space of potential research unlocked by this thesis.

It is the personal opinion of the author of this thesis that the main contribution of this thesis is the provision of a sound fundament that can be extended to provide a truly meaningful improvement in the practical realm of the domain of human computer interaction.

7.3 Scientific Challenges

The main scientific challenge during the preparation of this thesis was the process of structuring the findings during the conducted research into a sensible model that promises to be of practical value while fulfilling the goals initially set out for it.

In hindsight many of the decisions and structural characteristics of the Reference Model for Interaction Oriented Systems seem self-evident and possibly provoke a perception of simplicity of the model. Should this perception really be invoked in the reader, then the author believes a crucially important element of success has been achieved, as probably nothing is more refraining from engaging in a model than a complicated and convoluted appearance. The structural clarity and apparent simplicity of the reference model for interaction oriented system - that the author believes has been achieved - has been a long journey that was paved with critical analysis, challenging every decision made, restructuring the model many times over and subjecting it as often as possible to the eyes of those unfamiliar with the actual model itself but the ability to provide critical feedback.

Another challenge for the author was the accumulation of knowledge in the three perspectives to a point sufficient enough of mirroring their essence in the perspectives of the model.

Finally, the author would like to thank the reader for the time invested in reading this document; if nothing else obviously at least this part.

Bibliography

[AMB+04] Alain Abran, James W. Moore, Pierre Bourque, Robert Dupuis, and Leonard L. Tripp. *Guide to the Software Engineering Body of Knowledge: 2004 Edition - SWEBOK.* IEEE, 2004.

[Ari91] Aristotle. *Metaphysics.* Oxford University Press, (1991).

[Bac10] Francis Bacon. *Novum Organum.* Forgotten Books, 2010.

[Bar88] Marie-France Barthet. *Logiciels interactifs et ergonomie.* Dunod Informatique, Paris, 1988.

[Buc68] Walter Frederick Buckley. *Modern Systems Research for the Behavioral Scientist.* Aldine Publishing Company, 1968.

[Bux07] Bill Buxton. *Sketching User Experiences: Getting the Design Right and the Right Design.* Morgan Kaufmann, 2007.

[Cha09] Robert Charette. Why software fails. http://bit.ly/7wVjq, June 2009.

[Che99] Peter Checkland. *Systems Thinking, Systems Practice: Includes a 30-Year Retrospective.* Wiley, 1999.

[CHI10] ACM CHI. Model-driven development of advanced user interfaces, August 2010.

[CNM83] Stuart K. Card, Allen Newell, and Thomas P. Moran. *The Psychology of Human-Computer Interaction.* L. Erlbaum Associates Inc., 1983.

[CRC07] Alan Cooper, Robert Reimann, and David Cronin. *About Face.* Wiley, 3rd edition, 2007.

[Dar93] Charles Darwin. *The Autobiography of Charles Darwin: 1809 - 1882*. Nora Barlow, 1993.

[Des37] Rene Descartes. *Discours de la méthode pour bien conduire sa raison, et chercher la vérité dans les sciences*. Rene Descartes, 1637.

[Dij82] Edsger W. Dijkstra. *Selected Writings in Computing: A Personal Perspective*. Springer-Verlag, 1982.

[Fly06] Bent Flyvbjerg. Five misunderstandings about case-study research. *Qualitative Inquiry*, 12(2):219 – 245, 2006.

[Gai81] Brian R. Gaines. The technology of interaction: Dialogue programming rules. *International Journal of Man-Machine Studies*, 1981.

[Gal07] Wilbert O. Galitz. *The Essential Guide to User Interface Design: An Introduction to GUI Design Principles and Techniques*. Wiley Publishing Inc., third edition edition, 2007.

[Inc06] Apple Inc. *Apple Human Interface Guidelines*, Oct 2006.

[Ins73] American National Standards Insitute. *American National Psychoacoustical Terminology*. American Standards Association, 1973.

[Jac01] Michael Jackson. *Problem frames: Analyzing and Structuring Software Development Problems*. Addison Wesley, 2001.

[JK96] B. E. John and D. E. Kieras. The goms family of user interfaces analysis technique: Comparison and contrasts. In *ACM Transactions on Computer-Human Interaction*, number 3, pages 320–351, 1996.

[Jr.85] Albert F. Case Jr. Computer-aided software engineerng (case): Technology for improving software development productivity. *DATA BASE*, 17(1):35–43, 1985.

[Knu74] Donald E. Knuth. Computer programming as an art. *Communications of the ACM 1974/Vol. 17, No. 12*, pages 667–673, 1974.

[Küh05] Thomas Kühne. What is a model? *Dagstuhl Seminar 04101, Dagstuhl*, 2005.

[Lan86] Keith Lantz. On user interface reference models. Technical report, Nov 1986.

[Lim04] Quentin Limbourg. *Multi-Path Development of User Interfaces*. PhD thesis, Universite Catholique de Louvain, Oct 2004.

[LM86] Gene Lynch and Jon Meads. In search of a user interface reference model: Report on the sigchi workshop on user interface reference models. *SIGCHI Bull.*, 18(2):25–33, Nov 1986.

[LV04] Quentin Limbourg and Jean Vanderdonckt. Usixml: A user interface descriptoin language supporting multiple levels of independence. In *Engineering Advanced Web Applications*, pages 325–338. Rinton Press, 2004.

[Mah03] Bernd Mahr. *Modellieren. Beobachtungen und Gedanken zur Geschichte des Modellbegriffs*. Horst Bredekamp, 2003.

[Mah08] Bernd Mahr. *Ein Modell des Modellseins - Ein Beitrag zur Aufklärung des Modellbegriffs*. Peter Lang Verlag, 2008.

[Mah09] Bernd Mahr. Information science and the logic of models. *Informatik Spektrum*, 32(3), 2009.

[Man05] Bernard Mandeville. *The Fable of the Bees: And Other Writings*. Hacket Publishing Company, 1997 (1705).

[Mar98] P. Marinis. *Hellenic World-Vision*. Nea Thesis Editions, 1998.

[MB79] Stephen McAdams and Albert Bregman. Hearing musical streams. *Computer Music Journal*, 3(4), 1979.

[ME68] Karl Marx and Friedrich Engels. *Karl Marx - Friedrich Engels - Werke, Band 23, Das Kapital, Bd. I*. Dietz Verlag, 1968.

[Met09] Wolfgang Metzer. *Laws of Seeing*. MIT Press, 2009.

[MK09] Rahul Mohan and Vinay Kulkarni. Model driven development of graphical user interfaces for enterprise business applications – experience, lessons learnt and a way forward. In *Model Driven Engineering Languages and Systems*. Springer, Berlin / Heidelberg, 2009.

[MM92]   J. L. Miller and J. G. Miller. Greater than the sum of its parts. i. subsystems which process both matter-energy and information. In *Systems Research and Behavioral Science*, volume 37, pages 1–9. Wiley, 1992.

[MMJS09]   M. Minovic, M. Milovanovic, M. Jovanovic, and D. Starcevic. Model driven development of user interfaces for educational games. In *Human System Interactions*, 2009.

[Mös93]   Hanspeter Mössenböck. *Objektorientierte Programmierung*. Springer-Verlag, 1993.

[Nor90]   Donald Norman. *The Design of Everyday Things*. Doubleday Business, 1990.

[Ols67]   Harry F. Olson. *Music, Physics and Engineering*. Dover Publications, 1967.

[Pal94]   Philippe Palanque. Petri net based design of user-driven interfaces using the interactive cooperative objects formalism. In *Proceedings of the 1st Eurographics Workshop on Design, Specification, and Verification of Interactive Systems*. DSV-IS, Springer-Verlag, 1994.

[Pan83]   Erwin Panofsky. *Meaning in the Visual Arts*. University of Chicago Press, 1983.

[PE99]   Angel Puerta and Jacob Eisenstein. Towards a general computational framework for model-based interface development systems. pages 171–178, Jan 1999.

[PEGM94]   Angel Puerta, Henrik Eriksson, John Gennari, and Mark Musen. Beyond data models for automated user interface generation. pages 353–366, 1994.

[Phi09]   Philips. Philips' brand promise. http://bit.ly/cXu6kd, June 2009.

[PlaBC]   Plato. Philebus. *Philebus*, 360 B.C.

[Pla07]   Plato. *The Republic*. Penguin Classics, 2007.

[PS97]   Angela Puerta and Pedro Szekely. A model-based interface development environment. *IEEE Softw.*, 14(4):40–47, Aug 1997.

[Ras94]   Jef Raskin. On user interface intuitivity. *Communications of the ACM 1994/Vol. 37, No. 9*, Nov 1994.

[Ras07]   Jef Raskin. *The Humane Interface*. Addison Wesley, 2007.

[Ree10] Trygve Reenskaug. Mvc xerox parc 1978-79. http://bit.ly/17ViZJ, May 2010.

[RG01] Robbins-Gioia. Robbins-gioia survey (2001). *Robbins-Gioia Survey (2001)*, 2001.

[RO97] RM-ODP. *RMODP Foundations*, Oct 1997.

[RO98] RM-ODP. *ISO/IEC 10746-1:1998(E) - (RM-ODP Overview)*, Nov 1998.

[RS08] Bernhard Rieder and Mirko Tobias Schäfer. Beyond engineering. *Beyond Engineering*, 2008.

[Sen94] Peter Senge. *The Fifth Discipline: The Art & Practice of the Learning Organization*. Doubleday Business, 1994.

[Sim80] Helen Simons. Towards a science of the singular: Essays about case study in educational research and evaluation. Technical report, University of East Anglia, Norwich: Centre for Applied Research in Education, 1980.

[Smi76] Adam Smith. *An Inquiry into the Nature and Causes of the Wealth of Nations*. W. Strahan and T. Cadell, London, 1776.

[Soy97] Susan K. Soy. The case study as a research method. University of Texas at Austin, 1997.

[SP00] Paulo Pinheiro Da Silva and Norman W. Paton. Umli: The unified modeling language for interactive applications. In *Proceedings of UML2000*, volume 1939 of LNCS, pages 117–132. Springer, 2000.

[SP03] Paulo Silva and Norman Paton. User interface modeling in umli. *IEEE Softw.*, 20(4):62–69, Jul 2003.

[SP05] Ben Shneiderman and Catherine Plaisant. *Designing the User Interface*. Addison Wesley, 4th edition edition, 2005.

[Sta73] Herbert Stachowiak. *Allgemeine Modelltheorie*. Springer-Verlag, 1973.

[Sta95] Robert E. Stakes. The art of case study research. Technical report, Thousand Oaks, CA, 1995.

[Sta08] Adrian Stanciulescu. *A Methodology for Developing Multimodal User Interfaces of Information Systems*. PhD thesis, Universite Catholique de Louvain, 2008.

[Stö10] Harald Störrle. Model driven development of user interface prototypes: an integrated approach. In *ECSA '10: Proceedings of the Fourth European Conference on Software Architecture*. ACM Press, New York, 2010.

[usi07] usixml.org. http://www.usixml.org, 2007.

[Van07] Jean Vanderdonckt. *UsiXML (USer Interface eXtensible Markup Language)*, Feb 2007.

[vB76] Ludwig von Bertalanffy. *General Systems Theory*. George Braziller Inc., 1976.

[Win71] Franz Winziger. *Dürer*. Hamburg: Rowohlt, 1971.

[Win96] Terry Winograd. *Bringing Design to Software*. Addison Wesley, 1996.

[Wor10] Princeton WordWebNet, June 2010.

[Yin84] Robert K. Yin. *Case study research: Design and methods*. Newbury Park, 1984.

Die VDM Verlagsservicegesellschaft sucht für wissenschaftliche Verlage abgeschlossene und herausragende

Dissertationen, Habilitationen, Diplomarbeiten, Master Theses, Magisterarbeiten usw.

für die kostenlose Publikation als Fachbuch.

Sie verfügen über eine Arbeit, die hohen inhaltlichen und formalen Ansprüchen genügt, und haben Interesse an einer honorarvergüteten Publikation?

Dann senden Sie bitte erste Informationen über sich und Ihre Arbeit per Email an *info@vdm-vsg.de*.

Sie erhalten kurzfristig unser Feedback!

VDM Verlagsservicegesellschaft mbH
Dudweiler Landstr. 99 Telefon +49 681 3720 174
D - 66123 Saarbrücken Fax +49 681 3720 1749
www.vdm-vsg.de

Die VDM Verlagsservicegesellschaft mbH vertritt

Printed by Books on Demand GmbH, Norderstedt / Germany